Protecting Wild Nature on Native Lands

Case Studies by Native Peoples from around the World

Volume I

Protecting Wild Nature on Native Lands

Case Studies by Native Peoples from around the World

Proceedings
1st Native Lands and Wilderness Council
Anchorage, Alaska
September 30–October 6, 2005

Editors

Julie Cajune
Confederation of Salish and Kootenai Tribes
Montana, U.S.A.

Vance G. Martin
The WILD Foundation
Colorado, U.S.A.

Terry Tanner
Confederated Salish and Kootenai Tribes
Montana, U.S.A.

THE
WILD.
FOUNDATION

The WILD Foundation
Boulder, Colorado U.S.A.

Fulcrum Publishing
Golden, Colorado U.S.A.

Library of Congress Cataloging-in-Publication Data

Protecting wild nature on Native lands : case studies by Native peoples from around the world / editors, Julie Cajune, Terry Tanner, Vance G. Martin.
    p. cm.
   ISBN-13: 978-1-55591-681-7 (alk. paper)
1. Native Lands and Wilderness Council. 2. Nature--Effect of human beings on--Case studies. 3. Indigenous peoples--Ecology--Case studies. 4. Indigenous peoples--Land tenure--Case studies. 5. Conservation of natural resources--Case studies. 6. Environmental protection--Case studies. 7. Environmental policy--Case studies. I. Cajune, Julie. II. Tanner, Terry, 1959- III. Martin, Vance.
  GF75.P76 2007
  333.95'16--dc22

2007039800

Printed in the United States of America by Color House Graphics, Inc.
0 9 8 7 6 5 4 3 2 1

Design by Patty Maher

Fulcrum Publishing
4690 Table Mountain Drive, Suite 100
Golden, Colorado 80403
800-992-2908 • 303-277-1623
www.fulcrumbooks.com

The WILD Foundation
P.O. Box 25027
Boulder, Colorado 80308
303-442-8811
www.wild.org
info@wild.org

Contents

Preface

In 1977, the 1st World Wilderness Congress (WWC) convened in apartheid-era Johannesburg, South Africa. South African–born conservationst Ian Player called the meeting. He had started The WILD Foundation in 1974 and by 1977 saw the need for a major international conservation gathering that would include, likely for the first time, indigenous people from Africa, North America, and Australia, who would share the platform with scientists and professional conservationists. Player also invited politicians, artists, business leaders, and managers who were vitally interested in conservation. He ignored South Africa's policy that such an interracial activity was illegal.

Academics and scientists among professional conservationists wondered at Player's idea of bringing such a mix of people together. Had he lost his marbles? Bankers? Artists? Indigenous people? He had not lost his marbles. It was just that the prevailing attitude of the political and academic conservation institutions at that time did not recognize the environmental knowledge, cultural history, acumen, and heightened preception of such people. As to indigenous people, perhaps only some field managers, wardens, and a very few others knew of and depended on the vast cultural heritage of those whose lands they worked on.

By 2004, the WWC had convened seven more times, meeting in Australia, the United Kingdom, the United States, Norway, India, and again in South Africa. The WILD Foundation, its partners, and colleagues continued to devise and implement plans to protect and sustain wilderness internationally. Each Congress produced practical results such as recommending new or expanded protected areas, new sources of funding, drafting better laws and policies, and targeting training, and more—in addition to a palpable, shared spirit of enthusiasm and commitment to wild nature. Naturally Congress participants included natives and community representatives from around the world, because collectively they control and manage vast areas of wildlands. They often work with little funding but with great traditional knowledge and with any modern technology they can lay their hands on to maintain their lands' essential wildness and to protect the critical services they provide.

At each successive WWC, WILD and its collaborators presented new issues pertinent to native approaches to conservation and integrated them with conservation practice and policy of the non-native conservation world. The result of this work was evident at the 8th WWC held in Anchorage, Alaska, in 2005. One of the five cochairs of the Congress was Byron Mallot, a Tlingit from southeastern Alaska, and some 15 percent of the delegates were native peoples from many countries. Almost 20 percent of the plenary program involved native delegates. In addition, a significant session held at the same time was the 1st Native Lands and Wilderness Council (NLWC). The idea was conceived by Terry Tanner of the Confederated and Salish and Kootenai in Montana, and convened by Tanner and his cochairs Ilarion Merculieff, an Aleut from the Bering Sea Council of Elders in Alaska, and Herb Norwegian, Grand Chief of the Dehcho, First Nations in Canada's Northwest Territories.

Tribal representatives from twenty-five nations attended and heard twelve case studies by natives managing and using their tribal and communal lands to protect wilderness and its associated cultural and biological values. Ten of the case studies are contained in this volume, one of the first of its kind to present articles by native people managing wild nature on their own lands.

The 1st NLWC was a pioneering initiative by native people to expand and strengthen the international movement of native communities to save their wildlands while saving their cultures. Their efforts are often characterized by significant challenges of funding and lack of equipment and infrastructure necessary to manage what are often vast tracts of wild land and seas. However, what impresses me is the undeniable link between the health and biological integrity of these ancestral wildlands and the strength of traditional cultures still present remaining on them. Generally, there is a higher percentage of land management success on lands managed by traditional communities rather than on ancestral lands where indigineous people have been forced off or have voluntarily left to live elsewhere.

The WILD Foundation values, salutes, and promotes our friends and expert colleagues in traditional communities around the world. We also thank Ken Wilson and The Christensen Fund, the Ford Foundation, the Canadian International Development Agency, and the New York Community Trust for their vision and financial support that made it possible for us to help create and host the 1st Native Lands and Wilderness Council. Plans are currently underway for a Native Lands and Wilderness Council focusing on North America, which will lead up to an expanded 2nd NLWC at the 9th World Wilderness Congress to be held in Mexico in November 2009.

If wild nature and human society are to survive on this beautiful but beleaguered planet, it can only be through the combined effort of all people working to keep wildlands intact and biologically integrated. This rare but profoundly simple attitude respects the spirit of wild nature, recognizes its 3-million-year-old influence on human evolution, and honors its essential role in shaping human culture.

Vance G. Martin,

President, The WILD Foundation,

Boulder, Colorado,

May 2008

Introduction

~~~~~~~~~~~~~~~

Native Lands and Wilderness Council: Working for Wilderness, Wildlands, and Native People

Our story begins when the Creator put the animal people on the earth. He sent Coyote and Fox ahead as the world was full of evils and not yet fit for mankind. Coyote came with his brother Fox, to this big island, as the elders call this land, to free it of these evils. They were responsible for creating many geographical formations and providing good and special skills and knowledge for man to use. Coyote, however, left many faults such as greed, jealousy, hunger, envy and many other imperfections that we know of today.

—Clarence Woodcock
Confederated Salish and Kootenai Tribes
Montana, U.S.A.

This narrative, above, by the late Clarence Woodcock describes a sacred landscape that was the homeland of the Salish and Pend d'Oreille people in what is now Montana and western Canada. The landscape furnished the people with everything they needed, and their rich oral history informed their relationships and interdependence with it. Facing theft and invasion of tribal lands, disease, and a tidal wave of change, Salish and Pend d'Oreille leaders saved a remnant of their homeland. Within this remnant, the tribes set aside a wilderness area encompassing almost 32,000 hectares (92,000 acres) on the Flathead Indian Reservation in the Mission Mountains of Montana.

Terry Tanner grew up in the context of both generational loss and preservation. Cultural ancestors passed down the responsibility of land stewardship, and Tanner's life has been devoted to carrying out this responsibility. His vision of a Native Lands and Wilderness Council began here on the Flathead Indian Reservation with the commitment of the Confederated Salish and Kootenai Tribes to protect and manage their wilderness.

Tanner believes that stewardship of the land is a responsibility shared by all indigenous people. This belief fueled his dream of gathering people from around the world to share the stories of their land and how they are trying to keep it wild. He felt that land management and protection strategies could inform and inspire them. This was Tanner's vision when he spoke at the 7th World Wilderness Congress in 2004 in South Africa.

Through generous funding from The WILD Foundation, The Christensen Foundation, The Ford Foundation, and others, Tanner's dream was realized. The 2005 World Wilderness Congress convened in Anchorage, Alaska, with a Native Lands and Wilderness Council (NLWC) that hosted indigenous people from Mexico, Canada, Australia, Mozambique, the Congo, Brazil, Guyana, Colombia, and elsewhere. Tribal people shared stories of remarkable conservation work in their communities, often in the face of constant threat. Other stories chronicled the loss of control over land. I will not forget Kabo Hendrick Mosweu's poignant description of the marginalized San people dispossessed of their aboriginal land title and displaced throughout Botswana, South Africa, Namibia, Angola, Zambia, and Zimbabwe.

As the Congress concluded and the NLWC came to a close, participants shared stories and songs and prayers. In this moment, we were reminded that protecting our land is paramount in preserving our life, our culture, and our spirituality. We also understood how essential our voices—the voices of indigenous people—are to the guidance and efforts of conservation in the twenty-first century.

The case studies that follow are the stories of indigenous communities working to protect their lands. These communities control their lands and have made the conscious decision not to develop them for commercial resource extraction. They have a stated desire to keep their lands as pristine as possible. At times this is done at a great cost to the people's prosperity. These stories are heroic.

Julie Cajune,
Confederated Salish and Kootenai Tribes,
Pablo, Montana

Chapter 1

The Mission Mountains Tribal Wilderness Area, U.S.A.

Terry Tanner,

Confederated Salish and Kootenai Tribes,

Pablo, Montana

The area known today as the Mission Mountains Tribal Wilderness was a small part of a vast landscape that our people have cared for from time immemorial. We are connected spiritually and physically to this place, tied to this land by our ancestors' and elders' stories that relate our oral history. John Stanislaw, tribal elder, told me that every drainage, every lake, and every mountain, valley, and prairie have a significant story.

Today, we still depend on this land for our game, our fish, and our plants. The elders have told us how important it is to protect it. We not only have to protect the Mission Mountains Wilderness, but we have to watch over all of the places in our aboriginal territory. Our ancestors kept our rights to continue our relationship with our homelands in the 1855 Treaty of Hellgate. We honor our ancestors through our stewardship of the land and by maintaining and exercising the rights we kept in our treaty. This is our generational responsibility that we grow up with as Indian people.

—Terry Tanner, Wildland Recreation Program,
Confederated Salish and Kootenai Tribes

Editor's Note: Terry Tanner presented this case study, basing it on his work and that of David Rockwell, a 1999 paper compiled by Tom McDonald and Lester Bigcrane on behalf of the Confederated Salish and Kootenai Tribes through the University of Montana's Distance Learning Program.

History: The First Tribal Wilderness

The striking peaks found in the Mission Range of the Flathead Nation of western Montana crown a wilderness rare in the United States both in majesty and management.

Just south of Flathead Lake, the range rises more than a mile above the farmlands and towns of the Mission Valley; the western front of the range provides one of the most spectacular valley landscapes in the Rocky Mountain region. But the range is more than a natural wonder. It is the first place in which an Indian nation has matched, and possibly exceeded, the U.S. Federal Government in dedicating lands to be managed as wilderness.

The Confederated Salish and Kootenai Tribes are composed of descendants of Salish (Flathead), Pend d'Oreille, and Kootenai Indian tribes that traditionally occupied 8 million hectares (20 million acres) stretching from central Montana, across the Idaho Panhandle to eastern Washington, and north into Alberta, Saskatchewan, and British Columbia, Canada. The Hellgate Treaty of 1855 ceded the majority of those ancestral lands to the U.S. Government in return for the approximately 0.5 million hectares (1.2 million acres) now known as the Flathead Indian Reservation.

In the words of Isaac Stevens, then governor of the Washington Territory, the treaty gave access to "much valuable land and an inexhaustible supply of timber" and enabled settlers "to secure titles to land and thus the growth of towns and villages." The loss of this vast wilderness meant the potential loss of traditional Indian society. Every aspect of the Indian culture, from hunting and food gathering to religious practices, depended upon a wilderness setting.

To the Salish, Pend d'Oreille, and Kootenai Indians, the Mission Range was one part of this wilderness homeland, distinct in its incredible ruggedness and extreme weather but no more wild or primeval than anywhere else. The Mission Range influenced the culture and economy of the tribes. The area could be crossed only through certain passes on a network of trails that had been used for thousands of years by the Salish, Pend d'Oreille, Kootenai, and other tribes. They enjoyed the striking natural beauty, fished the lakes, hunted elk, deer, goats, and sheep, and harvested plants from the forests and ridgetops. They also practiced spiritual traditions throughout the area.

The first attempt by the tribes to officially protect the Mission Range occurred in 1936, during a period of extensive trail construction in the mountainous areas of the reservation by the Indian Civilian Conservation Corps. That year the Tribal Council voted to set aside about 100,000 acres of the western slope of the Mission Range as an Indian-maintained national park. The tribes sought to retain ownership of the lands but planned to parallel the National Park Service in its administration of the area. With support of the local Bureau of Indian Affairs (BIA) superintendent, the council wanted to encourage tribal member use of the park. They envisioned an area of traditional encampments and opportunities for Indian guides to bring visitors into the park.

In a 1936 press release, the BIA superintendent of the Flathead Agency wrote:

> It is planned to maintain the park in its present natural state. Roads will not be built. … A complete system of trails will be, and some trails are already constructed. … These trails will, for the most part, follow old Indian trails. At natural camp places, shelters will be erected for the convenience of the traveler and explorer, with corrals in connection where necessary. Indian guides will be available to conduct parties through the park.

Ironically, just one year later, John Collier—then commissioner of Indian Affairs—signed an order drafted by then chief forester Bob Marshall for the same Bureau of Indian Affairs office that classified the Mission Range as a roadless area. The order established twelve such roadless areas and four wild areas on twelve reservations across the country. Its stated purpose: "If on reservations, where the Indians desire privacy, sizeable areas are uninvaded by roads, then it will be possible for the Indians of these tribes to maintain a retreat where they may escape from constant contact with white men."

A second goal was to preserve some untouched land for future generations. But because the federal government established the areas without consent of the tribes, the affected nations petitioned to have them declassified. The Confederated Salish and Kootenai formally protested the Marshall Order in 1939, and in 1958 they officially requested that the part of the order applying to the Flathead Reservation be withdrawn. The Mission Mountains Roadless Area was declassified in the *Federal Register* in 1959.

During the early 1970s, the Bureau of Indian Affairs' Flathead Agency proposed logging portions of the remaining roadless area on the western front of the range. The proposal, as well as other development activities (roads, pipelines, dams, and the like) fueled a renewed interest in preserving the Mission Range.

It was about this time that Thurman Trosper, a tribal member, retired U.S. Forest Service employee, and recent past president of the Wilderness Society, returned to the Flathead Reservation and proposed establishing a tribal wilderness area to the council.

Three Yayas

In 1974, as the Tribal Council was considering a proposal to log Ashley Creek in the heart of the Mission Range, three greatly respected grandmothers (*yayas*), Annie Pierre, Christine Woodcock, and Louise McDonald, protested the proposed timber sales and went to the council, accompanied by Germaine White, a Salish woman active in tribal and political affairs. The yayas requested a moment of the council's time to talk about a timber sale on Ashley Creek. The council agreed and each of the grandmothers spoke.

They said that people are only on earth for a short time, and that it is important to take care of what's here and to pass it on to the children in good condition. They said that this work was our responsibility, and that the Mission Mountains were a treasure. The Tribal Council listened, and when the last of the yayas had spoken, the chairman thanked the grandmothers and waited for them to sit down. But the grandmothers continued to stand. So the chairman asked if there was anything else they wanted to say. One of the yayas replied, "Well, we'll just wait here until you vote."

It soon became clear the women were not leaving, so finally the chairman called for a vote. That was the end of the Ashley Logging Unit, and the Ashley Creek sale was the last timber sale proposed within what would become the Mission Mountains Tribal Wilderness.

The grandmothers opened the way for community leaders to organize the Save the Mission Mountains Committee, led by tribal businessman Doug Allard. The committee circulated a petition in 1975 asking the council to designate the range as a tribal primitive area in which logging would be banned. Soon after this, the council seriously began to consider some type of wilderness protection.

Allard's Committee proposed a boundary that came to the base of the mountain range and included private and roaded lands, making it politically unfeasible. The Committee's interest, however, centered on protecting aesthetic values and preserving the wilderness character of the area, thereby retaining some of the cultural and spiritual values important to tribal members.

In 1976, the Tribal Council, at the recommendation of Thurman Trosper, contracted with the Wilderness Institute of the University of Montana to draft boundary and management proposals for a Mission Mountains Tribal Wilderness Area. Two years later, the institute presented the drafts—a compromise of previous proposals—to the council for review. The council took no immediate action, but a year later they approved the proposed boundary and created a new tribal program to oversee interim management of the area. Titled the Wildland Recreation Program, it was charged with developing a wilderness management plan to meet specific needs and values of the tribes.

The plan was completed in the spring of 1982. On June 15, the council approved Ordinance 79A, the Tribal Wilderness Ordinance, and adopted the Mission Mountains Tribal Wilderness Management Plan.

The Mission Divide makes up the eastern boundary of the Flathead Reservation; the east side of the Mission Range is managed by the U.S. Forest Service. In 1931, a portion of the range was classified as a primitive area. The "Mission Mountains Primitive Area" encompassed 27,000 hectares (67,000 acres). An additional 3,400 hectares

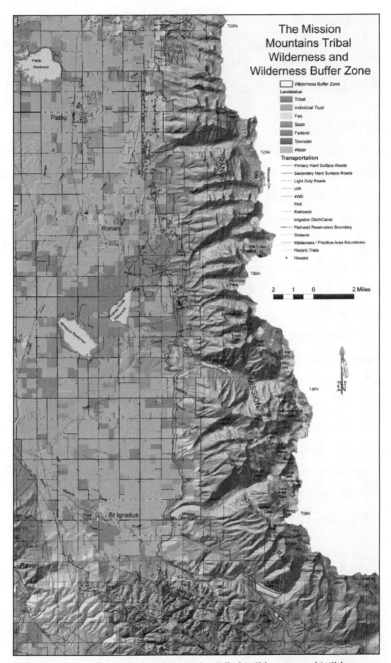

Fig. 1.1. A map of the Mission Mountains Tribal Wilderness and Wilderness
Buffer Zone. Courtesy of the Consolidated Salish and Kootenai Tribes

(8,500 acres) was added in 1939. Officially classified as wilderness in 1975, the 29,897-hectare (73,877-acre) area is now managed in accordance with the federal Wilderness Act (1964). A high level of cooperation exists between managers of the tribal and federal areas.

Tribal Ordinance 79A

The Mission Mountains Tribal Wilderness as established by Tribal Ordinance 79A in June 1982 Article II of the Constitution and Bylaws of the Confederated Salish and Kootenai Tribes provides that "all final decisions of the Tribal Council on matters of general and permanent interest to the members of the Confederated Tribes shall be embodied in ordinances."

But ordinances are not permanent enactments; they can be revised or rescinded by a simple majority vote of the council. However, popular support for wilderness would make it difficult for the Tribal Council to rescind the ordinance or weaken its provisions. The only stronger protection than the current ordinance is an ordinance passed by the council and approved by the tribal membership, an option a future council may consider.

The Tribal Council's 1982 approval of Ordinance 79A was historic. It was the first time that an Indian tribe decided on its own accord to protect a sizable portion of its lands as wilderness, and to provide policy and personnel to fulfill its purpose. It states:

> Wilderness has played a paramount role in shaping the character of the people and the culture of the Salish and Kootenai Tribes; it is the essence of traditional Indian religion and has served the Indian people of these Tribes as a place to hunt, as a place to gather medicinal herbs and roots, as a vision seeking ground, as a sanctuary, and in countless other ways for thousands of years. Because

maintaining an enduring resource of wilderness is vitally important to the people of the Confederated Salish and Kootenai Tribes and the perpetuation of their culture, there is hereby established a Mission Mountains Tribal Wilderness Area and this area, described herein, shall be administered to protect and preserve wilderness values.

Because of the precedent-setting nature of the designation, no widely-recognized legal definition of wilderness existed at the time other than that of the 1964 federal Wilderness Act. The language of the tribal ordinance, particularly the definition of wilderness, matches that of the federal act:

A wilderness is hereby recognized as an area where the earth and its community of life are untrammeled by man, where man himself is a visitor who does not remain. An area of wilderness is further defined as an area of undeveloped tribal land, retaining its primeval character and influence, without permanent improvements or human habitation, which is protected and managed so as to preserve its natural conditions.

It is the principal objective of this Ordinance to protect and preserve an area of land in its natural conditions in perpetuity. This Wilderness shall be devoted to the purposes of recreational, scenic, scientific, educational, conservation, cultural, religious and historical use only insofar as these uses are consistent with the spirit and provisions of this Ordinance. Human use of this area must not interfere with the preservation of the area as wilderness.

A significant difference between the Tribal Ordinance and the federal Wilderness Act is that Ordinance 79A states that a primary purpose of the Mission Mountains Tribal Wilderness is the preservation of tribal culture, and it acknowledges the importance of wilderness to the perpetuation of traditional Indian religion.

The authors of the ordinance may have borrowed from the federal wilderness language, but they also consulted cultural and spiritual leaders within the tribal community. Although there is a strong belief that traditional Indian culture is part of the natural world, the consensus was that the value of the Mission Range would be substantially diminished if any human use was allowed to degrade the area's exceptional natural qualities. They were especially concerned about the affects of non-Indian use and the impacts of twentieth-century technologies. In the end, they decided that preservation of the area as wilderness took precedence over human use.

In that spirit, the ordinance prohibits permanent structures and building roads in the wilderness

> except as necessary to meet the minimum requirements for administration of the Area for the purpose of this Ordinance (including measures required in emergencies involving the health and safety of persons within the area), there shall be no temporary road, no use of motor vehicles, motorized equipment or motorboats, no landing of aircraft or other form of mechanical transport, and no structure or installation within the area.

The Plan and How Management Sets This Wilderness Apart

Management is necessary to ensure an enduring wilderness in the Mission Mountains. The manager's job is to monitor human uses and their influences, to identify how they are affecting or changing natural processes, to define the limits of acceptable human-caused change, and then to act in a manner consistent with the purpose of the Wilderness.

The Mission Mountains Tribal Wilderness is located on the western slopes of the Mission Range and covers nearly 37,000 hectares (92,000 acres). It ranges in elevation from 1,200 meters (4,000 feet) to over 3,000 meters (10,000 feet), and is about 55 kilometers (34 miles) long and 8 kilometers (5 miles) wide.

On the eastern slope of the range, the U.S. Forest Service manages the federally protected Mission Mountains Wilderness, established in 1975 and covering approximately 30,000 hectares (75,000 acres). Both wilderness areas combine with the 1-million-acre Bob Marshall Wilderness to form one large ecosystem. Geographic features include forested slopes and high mountain valleys, rocky cliffs, rugged rocky peaks, subalpine and alpine lakes, creeks, and some small glaciers.

On the tribal side—the west side—the forest cover is dominated by Douglas fir and subalpine fir trees mixed with cedar, larch, spruce, ponderosa pine, and lodgepole pine. The Douglas fir communities on the lower slopes are proceeding toward climax stage; some stands are quite dense, resulting in increased outbreaks of insect infestations and disease, high mortality, blowdown, and buildup of fire fuels.

Nine major streams issue from the Mission Mountains Tribal Wilderness Area, and nearly 115 lakes can be found in the cirques created by the glaciers that shaped the landscape. In the past, campsites along these lakes were used for Indian hunting and fishing or as rest stops during journeys across the mountains. These high mountain lakes provide breathtaking and memorable sights. Unfortunately, some have been degraded by excessive or inappropriate use, which has caused soil compaction and erosion, and created litter, multiple fire rings, and horse and human fecal contamination of surface waters.

Most trailheads are located at the wilderness boundary. Some have campground facilities; others are marked only by a sign. Many of the trails were built by the tribes long ago; others were built by the Civilian Conservation Corps (CCC) in the 1930s.

The number of trails and trailheads has varied through the years. A 1941 CCC inventory counted twenty-six trailheads and forty trails; a 1963 inventory listed twenty trailheads and twenty trails; and a 1972 inventory reported only six trailheads and eight trails. Today, there are nine developed trailheads and twelve major trails that are maintained and regularly used. An additional eight trails receive limited use and receive only impact maintenance.

The primary season of use is from June to September, although higher trails and lakes are not used until midsummer after the snow-pack melts. The trails are all in prime wildlife habitats. Grizzly bears, elk, deer, mountain lions, mountain goats, eagles, black bears, and other wildlife create special management needs.

Numerous roads lead to the wilderness boundary along the foothills of the Mission Range. County roads, private roads, irrigation roads, power line access roads, and old tribal logging roads crisscross the landscape at and near the base of the mountains. Many private and tribal (BIA logging) roads run within the buffer zone and in some cases into the wilderness. All roads within the wilderness have been ordered closed, however some remain open due to closure logistics. These roads are sometimes used for illegal activities such as cutting Christmas trees and harvesting fuel wood, hunting by nonmembers, and vehicle use without appropriate permits.

Management Plan Objectives

The wilderness is currently managed under the Mission Mountains Tribal Wilderness Management Plan, revised in 1997, for the "protection and preservation of the area's natural conditions in perpetuity." Management of the area enables the tribes to monitor human uses and their influences, define limits of acceptable change, and act to prevent degradation and restore impacted areas. The Wilderness Plan is an administrative guide for tribal staff and the framework for human use of the area.

The Tribal Wilderness Ordinance provides for human uses as long as they are consistent with the area's primary purpose: the protection and preservation of natural conditions in perpetuity. The protection of the wilderness resource is the dominant motivation in all management decisions. As defined by the ordinance, wilderness has many elements to be considered in management of the area. Management seeks to treat the wilderness as a whole and not as a series of separate, distinct parts.

Also inherent in the ordinance is the recognition that, in addition to the benefits derived from the direct use of the area as wilderness, there are substantial indirect benefits to many tribal members. That is, tribal members draw spiritual and physical refreshment from knowing that the area, its plants, and its wild animals are protected.

The manager's job is to monitor human uses and their influences, to identify how they are affecting or changing natural processes, to define the limits of acceptable human-caused change, and to act in a manner consistent with the purpose of wilderness—prioritizing the protection of biodiversity, nature-based cultural history, and solitude and spiritual renewal—in an increasingly crowded and technological world. The policies contained within the plan define the limits of acceptable human-caused change.

Management strives to maintain or, in special cases, reestablish natural distributions and numbers of plants and animals. Except as specifically provided for in the ordinance, natural physical and biological processes are allowed to continue without human influence.

Management also seeks to preserve spontaneity of use and as much freedom from regulation as possible, while preserving the

Fig. 1.2. Tribal horsemen in what was to become the Mission Mountains Tribal Wilderness Area. Courtesy of the Confederated Salish and Kootenai Tribes

naturalness of the wilderness area. It emphasizes solitude, physical and mental challenge, and freedom from the intrusion of unnatural sights and sounds. Indirect methods of distributing use are favored over direct regulation.

In addition, management seeks to provide visitors with a spectrum of wilderness opportunities, ranging, for example, from a good selection of well-maintained trails to areas without trails. Another objective is to prevent further degradation of naturalness and solitude and to restore heavily impacted, substandard areas.

Management is carried out in the least obtrusive manner possible. For example, tools used are the minimum necessary to safely and successfully do the work. The tool, equipment, or structure chosen is the one that will least degrade wilderness values, whether temporarily or permanently.

The Mission Mountains Tribal Wilderness is managed as a tribal wilderness, and the needs and values of tribal members take precedence over those of nontribal members. A common thread through all management considerations is the tribes' cultural and spiritual ties to wilderness.

Although wilderness use trends may vary, the simple existence of wilderness in a region has economic benefits. Population growth over the past fifteen years in counties adjacent to wilderness areas has been two to three and a half times higher than in other counties, according to a study of 277 U.S. counties. In Montana during the 1980s, nine of the top twelve counties in population growth were located next to wilderness areas. These "wilderness counties" became "magnets to business and population because of the high quality local environmental resources, many of which are preserved and protected by wilderness." (Gundar Rudzitis, "How Important Is Wilderness," 4th World Wilderness Congress, Estes Park, Colorado,1987) These counties grew economically in spite of fluctuations in the national economy because the natural landscape "drew people there, kept them there, and helped them permanently sustain the local communities and economies." (Thomas Power, *The Economic Pursuit of Quality*, New York: M. E. Sharpe, 1988)

Continuous impacts on limited wilderness resources by human and livestock use have made it necessary to restrict certain activities in some parts of the wilderness. Several zones in the Mission Mountains Tribal Wilderness receive special management considerations:

Special Grizzly Bear Management Zone: Established in 1982 along with and within the Tribal Wilderness, it covers approximately 4,000 hectares (10,000 acres) surrounding McDonald Peak and Ashley Lakes drainage. It is where, during the summer months, a number of grizzly bears gather to feed on insects. Each year from July 15 to October 1 the entire area is closed to human use to both minimize disturbance to bears and provide visitor safety.

Ashley Lakes Day Use Area: The Ashley Lakes area and trail, located within the Special Grizzly Bear Management Zone, is restricted to day use when the area is open to recreational use. During spring and fall, this area may receive heavy grizzly bear use and there is a potential for human-bear conflicts. This restriction is designed to both minimize disturbance to bears and to provide for the safety of people.

Trailless Area: When the Tribal Wilderness was established, this area had no trails. It has not been economically feasible to develop new trails in this rugged and rocky terrain, and the country was open enough to make trails unnecessary. The area provides a wider spectrum of opportunities in cross-country travel, a greater chance to experience solitude, and generally more primitive and wild camping and hiking experiences.

Spring Stock Use Closure: Every year since 1989, from March 1 through June 30 the entire Tribal Wilderness area has been closed to livestock use, including all pack and riding stock. This closure addresses the damage and erosion problems caused by livestock when soils are most vulnerable.

North Fork Post Creek Fishing Closure: Enacted in 1989 to protect naturally reproducing trout populations in the Summit Basin area from fishing harvest, this regulation affords protection to spawning runs in the tributary streams of Moon, Long, Frog, and Summit Lakes.

The following areas and resources are given special consideration when decisions are made regarding management of wilderness resources:

- Grizzly Bear Management Zone and grizzly bear habitats,
- Other endangered species and habitats,
- Cultural site protection,
- Maintenance of fragile alpine/tundra ecosystem,

- Sensitivity of riparian zones for water quality and wildlife protection,
- Municipal watershed protection,
- Trailless area maintenance,
- Wilderness Buffer Zone,
- Trails and campsites, and,
- Fishery management, giving special attention to native West Slope cutthroat trout and bull trout.

The following provisions principally govern use by nontribal members:

- Use of any tribal lands or waters by nontribal members requires the purchase of a tribal conservation license with the appropriate activity stamp,
- A group size limit of eight persons and eight head of livestock is enforced within wilderness lands,
- Use of a campsite for longer than three consecutive days is prohibited,
- It is illegal to carry or use a firearm, and,
- Commercial use of the Tribal Wilderness is not allowed.

The following plans, policies, codes, and resolutions affect the wilderness:

- Ordinance 79A, Tribal Resolution 82-137;
- Mission Mountains Tribal Wilderness Management Plan;
- Mission Mountains Tribal Wilderness Buffer Zone Management Plan;
- Grizzly Bear Management Plan for the Flathead Reservation;
- Mission Mountains Tribal Wilderness Fire Management Plan;
- Fisheries Management Plan of the Flathead Indian Reservation;

- Reservation Class I Airshed Designation;
- Ronan municipal water supply lease (Middle Crow Creek);
- Snow Survey Measurement Agreement; and,
- Ordinance 44D subject to Joint Tribal/State Hunting & Fishing agreement.

In addition to the policies established by the tribes and the BIA, other agencies involved in management of similar resources adjacent to the Tribal Wilderness and Buffer Zone make an effort to standardize management goals. For example, the U.S. Forest Service is attempting to adopt the tribes' regulation limiting group size.

In 1992, the Confederated Salish & Kootenai Tribes and U.S. Department of Agriculture's Flathead National Forest developed a joint wilderness map for the Mission Mountains wilderness complex to increase visitor awareness of the tribal wilderness regulations and wildlife protection zones and to reduce visitor pressure on high-use areas.

The first Flathead Nation wilderness manager stated: "Wilderness is, to a segment of the tribal population, vitally important. It is one part of the Indian culture that remains as it was. Preservation, then, expresses reverence for the land and its community of life, as well as respect for Indian culture."

The Buffer Zone

The management goals of wilderness differ dramatically from the goals of nonwilderness. Land management strategies change abruptly at the Tribal Wilderness boundary, with impacts from activities occurring outside the wilderness encroaching, to some degree, on the wilderness. Accordingly, the Tribal Council decided to establish a buffer zone to act as a cushion to the Tribal Wilderness.

In January 1986, the Confederated Salish and Kootenai Tribal Council approved Resolution 86-47, which established the Wilderness Buffer Zone Committee, charged with drawing up a buffer zone boundary and management plan. Following council direction, the committee developed the overall goal "to protect and preserve the integrity of the Tribal Wilderness."

In 1987, the Tribal Council adopted the Mission Mountains Tribal Wilderness Buffer Zone Management Plan. In 1990, the Tribal Council approved Resolution 90-73, reestablishing the Buffer Zone Administrative Use Committee, that then revised the 1987 Mission Mountains Tribal Wilderness Buffer Zone Management Plan, which was adopted in 1993.

The Buffer Zone is designed to control, when possible, activities that may adversely impact the Tribal Wilderness. The intent is to establish interim tribal management practices for natural resources, not to represent an ultimate tribal governmental position on any one aspect of natural resource management. Rather, it deals with immediate management concerns in the least confrontational method possible, encouraging other jurisdictions and interested individuals to offer advice and suggestions on how to more fully address the issues.

The Buffer Zone encompasses nearly 9,300 hectares (23,000 acres) in the Mission Range foothills. The lower foothills are used for many purposes including cultural uses, livestock grazing, timber harvest, recreation, home sites, Christmas tree harvest, and post and pole harvest.

The objective of the Wilderness Buffer Zone Management Plan is to develop an administrative process that ensures the zone's management will use an interdisciplinary approach and consider all resources within the area. Additionally, the management plan provides clear guidelines for resource managers to follow when considering activities within the zone. It includes the following policies:

- All tribal, BIA, and other federal government programs conducting activities within the Buffer Zone will be governed by the guidelines set forth in the Wilderness Buffer Zone Management Plan;
- Private landowners and all nontribal governmental entities conducting activities within the Buffer Zone are encouraged to follow the guidelines in the Wilderness Buffer Zone Management Plan;
- The Administrative Use Oversight Committee (AUO) will be responsible for implementing and monitoring the Wilderness Buffer Zone Management Plan. The AUO will use an interdisciplinary approach and will call upon experts in appropriate fields as needs arise; and
- The Wilderness Buffer Zone Management Plan will be updated and amended as needed.

What Has Been Gained through Wilderness Designation

Tony Incashola, a cultural leader of our tribes, has said we protect these areas not for ourselves, but for our ancestors, our elders, and our children. Protecting the wilderness is a way of honoring our ancestors and elders, and a way of telling our children that we care about them and their future.

In our comprehensive resource plan, our tribes have identified the following fundamental commitments, based on long-held cultural attitudes toward the land:

- Respect and live in harmony with each other and with the land, which we are borrowing from our children,
- Act on a spiritual basis when dealing with the environment,
- Preserve the abundance of animals, plants, and fish, and
- Maintain hunting and fishing based on need and traditional use.

By establishing and maintaining the Tribal Wilderness, we help to sustain these deep-seated values, which are key to preserving our culture. Other, related benefits include:

- The Tribal Wilderness is an important retreat from roads, motorized vehicles, media, and all the other technologies and noises of modern society. It provides us with an appropriate place to connect with our ancestors and our traditional cultural and spiritual practices.

- For many tribal people, wilderness is a peaceful sanctuary that provides much-needed solitude and spiritual renewal. For other tribal members who may never visit the area, it puts their mind at peace to know that one of the most beautiful places on the Reservation is protected in its natural condition for this and future generations of tribal members and for the plant and animal communities.

- Our tribal communities depend on subsistence hunting and fishing close to home. Our spiritual traditions depend on sensitive species like grizzly bear, elk, mountain goat, wolf, lynx, and native trout. Those species in turn require undisturbed habitat to survive and thrive. Maintaining the Tribal Wilderness helps to preserve the diverse plant and animal life needed to keep tribal communities healthy.

- The reservation's cleanest water begins in the Tribal Wilderness and primitive areas. Tribal communities depend on clean water for drinking, fishing, spiritual and cultural traditions, agriculture, and a host of other uses.

- The Tribal Wilderness provides our youth with healthy alternatives for recreation. It is a place free of pressures like drugs and alcohol, a place where our young people can have extraordinary, even life-changing experiences while learning about their cultural and spiritual traditions.

- Designation of the Tribal Wilderness has made the Confederated Salish and Kootenai Tribes a national leader in the conservation movement and brought international respect and acclaim to the tribes. The recognition undoubtedly helped the tribes in their endeavor to assume management responsibility of the nearby National Bison Range.
- The Tribal Wilderness brings thousands of visitors to the reservation, many of whom spend money with tribal businesses.

Issues and Threats, Solutions and Approaches

By staying true to our values, remembering in our hearts who we are as Indian people—and reflecting that in how we protect tribal wilderness—we will be successful in passing on to our children something of value that is unique to our culture.

After the Tribal Council designated the Mission Mountains Tribal Wilderness and adopted a management plan, managers realized many of the greatest threats to the integrity of the wilderness were coming from activities occurring on lands adjacent or contiguous to the wilderness. They identified the following issues for areas both within and outside the tribal wilderness boundary:

- Homesite development on tribal and private lands,
- Methods of fire control and fuel management,
- Shifts in tree species composition and increasing forest density due to fire exclusion,
- Affects of recreation and other uses on fisheries and riparian zones,
- Livestock use and grazing practices,
- Commercial outfitting within the wilderness,

- Forest pest, disease, and weed management,
- Protection of sensitive grizzly bear habitats,
- Roads leading up to or entering the wilderness,
- Regulation and enhancement of recreational use and opportunities for the development and management of facilities
- Protection of cultural, spiritual, and historic sites, and
- Water quality for valley watershed.

Working closely with the Tribal Council and the tribal membership, managers have taken several approaches to addressing these issues. The most significant of these approaches include:

- Developing and supporting a strong wilderness management program to monitor use and restore impacted areas, coordinated with the activities of all Tribal programs and departments in the wilderness;
- Establishing the Mission Mountains Wilderness Buffer Zone to address threats to the wilderness from adjacent and contiguous lands;
- Coordinating with Lake County's land use planning efforts so that activities on private lands adjacent to the wilderness are compatible with the purposes of the wilderness;
- Working closely with the U.S. Forest Service on its management of the adjacent federally protected Mission Mountains Wilderness so that Tribal policies, regulations, and closures are adequately respected and enforced;
- Developing a wilderness fire management plan and a Reservation fire management plan;
- Creating a 4,000-hectare (10,000-acre) grizzly bear conservation area in the heart of the Mission Mountains to protect feeding grizzly bears;

- Developing a strong education program focused on residents living near the wilderness and visitors to the wilderness;
- Acquiring land adjacent to the wilderness as opportunities arise to protect sensitive species like grizzly bears; and
- Making additions to the wilderness through the forest planning process.

Acknowledgments

We acknowledge with gratitude the help of many people in preparing and publishing this case study, among them David Rockwell, Vance G. Martin and The WILD Foundation, and Ken Wilson and The Christensen Fund.

Fig. 1.3. A rugged peak in the Cabinet Range of the Mission Mountains. Courtesy of the Confederated Salish and Kootenai Tribes

Chapter 2

The Wind River Indian Tribes, U.S.A.

Don Aragon,

Executive Director,
Wind River Environmental Quality Commission,
Fort Washakie, Wyoming

Editor's Note: This paper was previously published in the *International Journal of Wilderness* 13:2 (August 2007), pp. 14–17

Indigenous Knowledge

The World Wilderness Congresses (WWCs) have always operated on the principle that indigenous knowledge and perspectives must be included in any wilderness discussion to ensure a full understanding of the wilderness concept. This is an excellent approach to the development and preservation of wilderness areas, especially those areas that are under the control of Native American Indian Tribes.

The Shoshone and Northern Arapaho tribes of the Wind River Indian Reservation, at Fort Washakie, Wyoming, both through their tribal religion and their cultures believe that everything is connected and related, and that the world's environment is one. The land, the water, the air, the wildlife and animals, and humans are all related and are one in the eyes of the Creator. What happens to anyone happens to all, be it good or bad.

Nearby U.S. Federal Agency Wilderness Areas

The Wind River Indian Reservation is surrounded by wilderness areas that are designated as part of the National Wilderness Preservation System. To the west is the Popo-Agie Wilderness, 101,870 acres (41,243 hectares), created in 1984. To the southwest of the reservation is the Fitzpatrick Wilderness Area, which is 198,525 acres (80,374 hectares) and was created in 1976. To the northwest of the reservation is the Washakie Wilderness, created in 1964. It is the largest wilderness area in the state of Wyoming, at 704,274 acres (285,131 hectares). The Washakie Wilderness Area is named after the historical leader of the Shoshone tribe, Chief Washakie. Beyond the Washakie Wilderness is the Teton Wilderness, which was also created in 1964 and totals 585,338 acres (236,979 hectares).

Indian Reorganization Act

The Indian Reorganization Act of 1934 (IRA), also known as the Wheeler-Howard Act, provided the tribes of the United States the opportunity to self-govern and to reduce the influence of and dependence on the Bureau of Indian Affairs (BIA) and the U.S. Congress. The act gave to the Indian tribes the power to control their own resources, to incorporate, and to hold final power of approval over the disposition of tribal monies and income-producing holdings. Even though the Wind River tribes rejected the federal government's IRA terms, the IRA program has meant continued gains in the strength of tribal governments, as well as a larger voice in dealing with the federal government. Many of the reforms in the IRA, such as tribal courts, have been adopted by the Wind River tribes, even though they rejected the constitutional option of the Wheeler-Howard Act.

Shoshone and Northern Arapaho Tribal Governance

The business council system has replaced the chief/council systems in both the Shoshone and Northern Arapaho tribes at Wind River, leading to the formation of the BIA-instituted Tribal Councils. Each tribe currently has a General Council composed of all members of the tribes and a Business Council of six members who deal with individual political and business affairs. The Joint Business Council of the Shoshone and Northern Arapaho tribes is made up of six Shoshone council persons and six Northern Arapaho council persons.

The body of the whole in each tribe, the General Council, is considered by the tribes as the sovereign political power within the tribal governments. Through the late 1920s and early 1930s, governmental agents sought to make the smaller representative councils, especially the Joint Business Council, the more influential. This effort to deemphasize the importance of input from the whole tribe was encouraged as part of an overall detribalization effort by the U.S. government, intended to disengage Indians from their traditional forms of government and to adopt the representative democracy of the larger culture. In some cases, this erosion of Indian culture and government may have been well-intentioned or a result of simple ignorance of tribal values. It has been extensively noted that detribalization was a conscious effort on the part of federal officials to eradicate traditional Indian ways in order to gain control over the tribes and to access the valuable resources and land owned by the tribes.

Over a period of years leading up to 1934, the tribes resisted the pressures of assimilative procedures instituted by reservation agents and embraced their own as they saw fit and which met their needs. For many years the federal agents continued to pressure the Wind River tribes to adopt the IRA and form a constitution. Time after time, the two tribes' General Councils voted the IRA down. This was extremely frustrating to the federal agents, but they could do nothing about it. To this day, neither tribe has adopted the IRA, and both continue with their General Councils as the supreme body of the tribes.

Creation of a Roadless Area

In the earlier part of the 1900s, the Shoshone and Northern Arapaho tribes saw a lot of activity on the Wind River Indian Reservation. In 1905 and 1906, they saw the reservation opened up to homesteading by non-Indians. This happened in the northeastern part of the reservation, where the federal government opened what they called surplus reservation lands for homesteading.

The so-called surplus lands were open areas left over after the Dawes General Allotment Act of 1887 divided up reservation lands into individual tracts for individual Indian families. The Dawes Act did much more than simply divide tribal lands among individual Indians. It also

played a role in determining how much land the tribes would keep and how much would be open to acquisition by others, what citizenship rights Indians would have (because the bill tied land ownership to citizenship), what authority would be vested in the tribe and what in the individual, whether treaties would be honored or broken, and other similar and far-reaching policy issues. Not all of these questions were explicitly stated in the Dawes Act. But, because

Fig. 2.1. Don Aragon at work on the Wind River Reservation, Wyoming, U.S.A. Courtesy of the Shoshone and Arapahoe Tribes

they were implicit in the terms of the act, the Dawes Act has had a greater impact on the history of the tribes and Indian culture than almost any other single piece of legislation.

Also, at this time in the history of the state of Wyoming, the federal government was seeking to open up highways from the southern parts of the state into the Yellowstone Park area. The eastern governmental administration felt it was important for the rest of the U.S. population to be able to travel to and see the greatness of the Yellowstone Park area and the grandeur of the Teton Range. The opening of this area would bring tourists, and the Wind River tribes were worried about their land and the invasion of tourism.

The federal government surveyed and planned a roadway over the mountains from the Wind River Reservation's northwest corner. From the small town of Dubois, Wyoming, this northwesterly roadway would pass over the Rocky Mountains at the Togwotee Pass area and drop down into Teton Park. The tribes witnessed this activity and felt that if they did not pass some kind of legislation to protect their wilderness areas, the government would build roads elsewhere over the Rocky Mountains, going through their lands. The tribes' concerns were presented to the governmental agents in the 1930s; the agents then worked with the tribes' wishes in creating a roadlesss area on the Wind River Indian Reservation. The creation of a roadless area set aside more than 188,000 acres (76,113 hectares) of mountainous alpine areas and, to this day, the tribes still strongly protect it and do not allow any kind of motor-vehicle access. No roads or trails have been built in this area and none are planned.

Ironically, the same kind of concerns and activities were happening on other Indian reservations, and their activity created twelve such roadless areas and four wild areas on twelve Indian reservations across the country. The stated purpose was: "If on

Figs. 2.2 and 2.3. Land management on the Wind River Reservation includes intensive resource use as well as wildlands. These photos show exploratory drilling for gas and oil (left) and large-scale protection farming (right). Courtesy of the Shoshone and Arapahoe Tribes

reservations, where the Indians desire privacy, sizable areas are un-invaded by roads, then it will be possible for the Indians of these tribes to maintain a retreat where they may escape from constant contracts with the white man."

The overall goal was to preserve some untouched land for future Indian generations. In most cases, the federal government established these areas without the consent of the tribes, and the affected tribes petitioned to have the areas declassified and redesignated as wilderness areas. The Wind River tribes did not have their roadless area declassified, nor has it been redesignated as a wilderness area; they left it the way it is, and they do not plan any kind of action in this area. At this time, the roadless area on the Wind River Reservation is classified as a Class II airshed (under the Federal Clean Air Act as amended in 1990), and the tribes have investigated the possibilities of having the airshed reclassified to Class I, which may happen in the near future.

The Wind River tribes worked with federal governmental officials and had the roadless areas set aside in 1934 and affirmed by the U.S. Congress in the same year. The Wind River tribal protection was taken well before the Wilderness Act of 1964, and the roadless area has been neither touched nor changed since the 1934 preservation by the tribes.

Industrial and Energy Development

In the state of Wyoming, the industrial development of the coal bed methane (CBM) gas and the development of ordinary natural gas drilling are serious threats to all the wilderness areas because of air pollution. The tribes have expressed their concerns about this energy development in Wyoming and on the Wind River Reservation.

The tribes have asked Devon Oil Corporation to complete a comprehensive environmental impact statement (EIS) to show the potential effects of CBM gas development on reservation lands. The EIS was being developed and was scheduled to be made public in 2006.

For the past sixty to seventy years, the Wind River tribes have depended on the extraction industries of oil and natural gas development as their bread and butter. This continues today on the reservation; the individual members of the two tribes share in the royalties that are derived from the oil and gas development. Because this is the main economy of tribes, they want the oil companies to be good partners and to protect the tribal lands the same way the tribes themselves have done. The most recent request for an EIS is the

Figs. 2.4 and 2.5. Two views of the Milky Lakes, high in the Wind River Range, in the tribal wilderness/wildland area and site of alpine water quality testing. Courtesy of the Shoshone and Arapahoe Tribes

second time the tribes asked an oil company to provide one on the reservation, which shows good stewardship by the tribes.

Conclusion

The Shoshone and Arapaho tribes of the Wind River Indian Reservation have stood up against the federal government requests for them to adopt a tribal constitution and become IRA tribes. The two tribes still govern themselves, as they have for hundreds of years. Their General Councils, made up of all enrolled members of the two tribes, still make the decisions and develop the pathways for Tribal Councils to follow.

Chapter 3

~~~~~~~~~~~~~~~~~~~~

Dehcho First Nations, Canada

Herb Norwegian,
Grand Chief Dehcho Dene,
Fort Simpson, Northwest Territories

The Dehcho is an area of 22 million hectares (54 million acres) located in the Northwest Territories of Canada on the Mackenzie (Dehcho) River, an area of mountains and boreal forest that is larger than many countries. The Dehcho First Nations are Dene people who have occupied their homeland since time immemorial. Some elders were born on the land and our Slavey language is still spoken. Traditional harvesting remains an important economic and cultural pursuit. There is great pressure for industrial development, including mining activity and a major gas pipeline. The land is of paramount importance to our people. Our rights are protected under section 35 of Canada's Constitution Act, and we are engaged in a process with the government of Canada to address the future of our land with a treaty.

Our wilderness conservation efforts began with a traditional area-mapping exercise, in which we consulted our people on the areas that were important to their traditional use. We then digitized that material using Western science. The resulting map showed core areas and connecting corridors that we wish to conserve for our people's traditional use and the protection of the land. We negotiated with the Canadian government for that area to be withdrawn from further industrial dispositions during our process. We are looking at a variety of legal instruments for permanent protection, including working with Parks Canada to have the entire South Nahanni watershed and Ram Plateau (an area of 3.6 million hectares/8.9 million acres) protected as an expanded national park, the Nahanni National Park, a World Heritage site, which we would jointly manage, under Canada's National Parks Act. This headwaters area is vital both to our water quality and to our culture.

The next step to protect our land is the Dehcho Land Use Planning Process. A draft of that process was released in June 2005. The plan would protect more than 50 percent of our territory in interconnected conservation zones, a figure that I believe is a good rule of thumb for all First Nations to pursue to ensure the future of the land and the wildlife that lives on it. Good management based on the balance of land use through special management zones, general use zones, and an infrastructure corridor can accommodate careful industrial activity. This is consistent with the Canadian Boreal Framework, to which we are a founding signatory. The Dehcho Land Use Planning Committee will consult on the plan in 2006. Then we will work with the Canadian government to see that the final land use plan with its protections is adopted for our land. We expect the entire Dehcho Process to be complete by March 2008.

Chapter 4

Seri Case Studies in Natural Resource Management in the Gulf of California Region: Sea Turtles and Desert Bighorn Sheep, Mexico

Gabriel Hoeffer and **Fernando Morales,**
Seri Tribe, Sonora, Mexico

Laura Monti,
Department of Applied Indigenous Studies,
Northern Arizona University,
Flagstaff, Arizona

This chapter considers two case studies of natural resource management by the Seri Indians in their territorial boundaries along the central coast and waters of the Gulf of California in Sonora, Mexico.

The sea turtle conservation project is part of the traditional management plan for the Sargento Estuary on the mainland coast. The desert bighorn sheep project is managed on Tiburon Island, through a special agreement with the Wildlife Program of the Secretaria del Medio Ambiente y Recursos Naturales (SEMARNAT). These case studies are compared and contrasted for effective strategies to protect habitat and species located within native territory, with different approaches to community involvement and wilderness utilization of the desert and sea.

The Gulf of California spans an area of 28.2 million hectares (69.7 million acres) of marine and coastal habitats in Mexico. The sea, hyper-saline lagoons, and estuaries of the gulf rank among the highest in the world for endemic species and different habitat types per area. The gulf area harbors 30 species of marine mammals, 875 tropical and temperate fish species, 5 species of sea turtles, 4,500 marine macro-invertebrate species, and 450 macro-algae species.

This region is so diverse because the gulf is in a zone where trop-ical and temperate ecosystems of the Pacific converge. Thus, the Gulf of California is home to a greater number of species than might be expected given its surface area. Also, its relative isolation has allowed new species to develop. A wide range of physical environments are evident, including rocky, sandy, and muddy coastlines, and mangrove swamps. Due to its complex topography, latitude, and oceanographic-atmospheric processes, the gulf has three distinct zones: upper, central, and southern. Each zone is extremely rich due to seasonal upwelling and advection by tidal currents. The central island zone is where the Seri Indian people currently live. This zone has the highest number of endemic narrowly restricted species per surface area of any region in North America and acts as a buffer for the mainland, as it did during El Niño events in 2002.

The Seri Indians, known as Comcáac in their own language, live on the western coast of the Gulf of California, which is the central coast of the state of Sonora. Their enduring habitation of the central gulf coast and islands began more than a thousand years ago and has continued uninterrupted to the present. They derive their livelihood as expert fishers, hunters, and gatherers. Their long tenure in the harsh environment is due in part to their sophisticated knowledge of the desert and sea; while the desert environment may be harsh, the sea provides them with an abundance of fish, sea turtles, clams, crabs, and scallops. Today, fishing is the most important economic activity of the Seri and other coastal dwellers. Other economic activities include basketry, small food-store management, and tourism.

Coastal and marine habitats in the gulf are under pressure from industrial fisheries, tourism, freshwater depletion, pollution and agrochemicals, and siltation due to poor watershed management. Unregulated practices endanger the coral and rocky reefs and the desert islands. Overexploitation of land resources, particularly of the ironwood tree (*Olyney tesota*) has weakened the Seri tourist economy, which formerly exported ironwood carvings to Alaska. In 1992, changes to the *ejido* (a communal land-sharing program) resulted in policies that are shaping the pattern of coastal growth and development, growth of the shrimp farming industry, and restructuring the land tenure of the region. The main export market influence comes often from one or two large corporations that financially support exploitation of gulf shrimp for exclusive export to the United States, leading to unsustainable and ecologically damaging fishing. The illegal intrusion of Mexican fishing enterprises into Seri territory and the exploitation of local natural resources are also major challenges, in spite of clear legal protection conferred by Mexican law.

The presidential decree in 1974 resulted in Article 4 of the constitution, which established the official sovereign territory of the Seri people, roughly one-sixteenth of their historic range. Articles 4 and 26 of the Mexican constitution establish a legal basis for the projection of customary uses and for the promotion of language and culture of Indian communities as ejido and communal groups.

The Seri governing bodies, structures, and cultural practices that promote conservation and sustainable use of the sea and land resources include the traditional government, Bienes Comunales, and the Council of Elders. The first two bodies manage the economic and social aspects of the tribe, while the Council of Elders is charged with establishing laws to protect the territory, habitat, and species.

Today, several cooperatives fish for crab, clams, scallops, and fish. The traditional system of land and marine management, *ihizitihim*, consists of an extended family stewardship system for hunting and fishing grounds. Collecting areas are based on family heritage in customary use areas. This system includes stewardship responsibilities with taboos based on traditional ecological knowledge and conservation.

Sea Turtle Conservation in the Infiernillo Channel

The sea turtle conservation project began in 1998 as part of the Para Ecologo training project, which takes a biocultural approach to species and habitat protection. The projects are sponsored by The Comcáac Tribal Government and Council of Elders and Northern Arizona University's (NAU) Center for Sustainable Environments with the Department of Applied Indigenous Studies. Groups of elders, biologists, and mapmakers brought Western and indigenous science together to train youth leaders in the protection and sustainable use of desert and sea territory resources. Projects included studies of coastal and migratory birds, plants, the desert tortoise, sea turtles, crabs, and scallops.

The sea turtle conservation project grew out of a one-year project designed to develop local stewardship and a traditional management plan for this marine and coastal species that is of economic, ecological, and cultural importance in the Sargento Estuary on the mainland coast. The project began by training Seri in natural resource management. More than seventy-five Seri from different sectors of the community participated in species inventories, mapping, and discussions to develop a management plan for the region. The 2005 graduating class of this program included women, who may be the first indigenous women trained as traditional ecologists in the region.

Two maps based on traditional uses of the Sargento Estuary region were created to identify vegetation zones, key habitat areas, and historic Seri campsites. These maps serve as reference points for Seri natural resource conservation planning in the Sargento area. A database of key economic, ecological, and culturally important species in the Sargento region was developed to serve as baseline information for ongoing conservation efforts. A draft traditional management plan was ratified by leaders and important players of the Seri community. The plan, which includes Seri traditional knowledge of the region, has the potential to protect marine and coastal species and habitats that are central to the function of the Sargento ecology, including blue crabs, sea turtles, sea grasses, and mangrove swamps. Ratification of the habitat management plan by the Mexican government will give the Seri recognition as the first tribe to enact their own science-based habitat protection and use plan on the Pacific Coast.

Options for economic diversification and sustainable use of marine resources are underway. This project is important because of the current climate of coastal development in the region. Aquaculture developers are discussing with community leaders about developing aquaculture in protected waters. The Infiernillo Channel and the Sargento Estuary are among the last protected areas on the mainland coast of the Gulf of California. The Sargento Estuary habitat complex is an essential stopover for migratory birds moving along the Pacific Flyway and is a nursery for key economic marine invertebrate and fish species. Large stands of cardón cactus (*Pachycereus pringilii*), valued by the Seri for their sweet fruit, occur along the *bajadas* (shallow slopes) of Tepopa Mountain. The coastal mountain that borders the estuary to the north provides habitat and nursery grounds to bighorn sheep, recently introduced as part of an effort to diversify the Seri economy.

Coastal lagoons, channels, and estuaries provide important feeding and developmental grounds for sea turtles. Five sea turtle species are known to occur in this region: the Eastern Pacific green turtle (*Chelonia mydas*), the Pacific loggerhead (*Carretta caretta*), the olive Ridley (*Lepidochelys olivacea*), the hawksbill (*Eretmochelys imricata*), and the leatherback (*Dermochelys coriacea*). Although sea turtle populations are affected by many types of natural mortality, human-related causes of death are a continuous concern worldwide. These factors include boat collisions, drowning in fishing nets, and ingestion of plastic. Turtles used as meat, whether caught intentionally or accidentally, also contribute substantially to the decline of many sea turtle populations.

In 1972, the Mexican government began to strictly regulate the capture of sea turtles (Secretatia de Pesca, 1990). Although laws now exist forbidding the capture or consumption of turtles, these laws are often difficult to enforce. Along the mainland coast of the Gulf, the majority of inhabitants are employed as fishermen who have limited economic alternatives. Sea turtles are historically considered a delicacy to be served on special occasions, thus the pressure to sell turtle illegally on the black market is strong. The sale of one turtle can be equivalent to more than a month's income for a fisherman during high season.

Regulation against sea turtle hunting and consumption has had a significant impact on Seri culture and fishing economy. In the past, sea turtle was an important source of protein during the spring and summer. Today, nutrition-related diseases such as diabetes and heart disease are the leading causes of illness and mortality in the communities, a reflection of the recent shift away from subsistence fishing in the communities.

The sea turtle, especially the leatherback turtle, remains a cultural keystone species in Seri culture. The sea turtle is an important entity in their creation stories. The elders teach that sea turtles understand the Seri language, and so they sing to the turtles to protect them and their offspring on long journeys. They believe that the survival of the sea turtle and the survival of Seri culture are intertwined. Both Seri youth and elders are championing conservation efforts throughout the Gulf region.

A sea turtle conservation program, the Grupo Tortugeuro Comcáac, is based on the elders' expert knowledge of the sea turtles' migration routes and foraging sites. In this way, they are able to monitor the turtles and shed light on the population dynamics of turtles that migrate to their region. Using specially adapted nets, the team is able to capture and study the animals and then release them with identification tags. In this way, they collaborate with a network of other conservation groups in the region to identify and protect nesting sites, migration routes, and forage areas. Permits to capture and release the turtles are obtained in collaboration with SEMARNAT and a marine biologist working in the region. The team monitors the coastline for carapaces of turtles caught accidentally or intentionally, and they promote sea turtle conservation through community education events. Ecotourism is now being explored as a way to sustain long-term monitoring and conservation efforts.

Desert Bighorn Sheep Recovery Project on Tiburon Island

Tiburon Island (Tahéöc) is the largest island in the Gulf of California, and is named for the schools of shark that prey on abundant small fish that forage in the surrounding waters. The island's coastal waters have the most extensive development of eelgrass of anywhere in the Gulf of California. The green turtle is extremely abundant as are mullet, crabs, oysters, and clams in the estuaries. Mule deer, desert tortoises, and jackrabbits are abundant on the island. It is considered the heartland of Seri culture and was inhabited by three distinct bands of Seri Indians. Seri families took refuge within the mountains of this island during invasions and persecution by the Spanish and then Mexican army beginning in the eighteenth through the twentieth century.

In the 1950s, the Mexican government established settlements with running water and housing on the mainland, and in 1963 this island was decreed a wildlife refuge and nature reserve. The designation was based on biological and ecological grounds and failed to consider the needs and demands of the Seri people. Twelve years later, in 1975, President Luis Echeverria directed the secretary of Agrarian Reform to give the Seri formal possession of Tiburon as part of ejido, a communal property allotment to the tribe under federal jurisdiction. This was the first recognition by the federal government of the Seri's right to their ancestral land. At that time, it was also decreed that the coastal waters were exclusively under the domain of members of the Seri tribe and their fishing cooperative, Sociedad Cooperative de la Produccion Pesquera; the coastal waters were off limits to other fishers (INE, 1993). In 1978, the island was included under the protected area of the islands of the Gulf of California and is considered a reserve and a refuge for migratory birds and wildlife (Gomex-Pompa, 1995). In 2000, the government Secretaria de Medio Ambiente y Recursos Naturales, in collaboration with the tribe, developed a management plan for the island. Managed natural resource extraction areas (UMAs) were approved during this process.

The initial purpose for protecting Tiburon in 1963 was to create a mule deer (*Odocoileus hemonus sheldone*) refuge to protect the species from extensive poaching by hunters from Sonora. At that time, the hunting by the Seri was considered a threat to the game species and part of the game conservation problem on the island. No hunting permits were granted to the tribe, and for two years (1975–1977) the marines of the Mexican navy had a permanent presence on the island and game wardens prohibited Seri from hunting on the island (Excurra et al., 2002).

Bighorn sheep (*Ovis canadensis Mexicana*), a Sonoran Desert subspecies, were introduced in 1975 as part of a federal program to study and protect bighorn in Sonora under the management of the Secretaria de Agricultura y Recursos Hidraulicos (SARH), the Secretary of Agriculture and Water Resources, an agency of the federal government. The bighorn sheep transplant was successful; by 1999, their population had grown to more than 600 animals, estimated through aerial census.

Scientists from the National Autonomous University of Mexico (UNAM) launched an ambitious project to study and manage the bighorn sheep project. The Seri governor at the time, Pedro Romero, led the Seri collaboration agreements. Don Romero, now deceased, was a visionary thinker and foresaw the potential economic and social benefits of the project. The Arizona Game and Fish Department and staff from two conservation organizations, Unidos para la Conservacion and Agrupacion Sierra Madre, surveyed and studied the bighorn population. This led to a sport hunting project funded by American hunters; international auctions of hunting permits generated bids for permits. Half of these funds support research by UNAM's scientists and for conservation and management actions for the bighorn sheep population on Tiburon. The other half goes directly to the Seri tribe. A regulated number of permits are issued each year based on bighorn population and plant ecology studies.

The Tiburon bighorn sheep project contributes substantially to the conservation of bighorn sheep on mainland Mexico by providing animals to repopulate former bighorn distribution ranges in Sonora, Chihuahua, Coahuila, and Nuevo Leon, and generates income for the Seri people.

In addition to diversifying the Seri economy, the project has provided training and jobs: The hunting activities are led by a team of Seri, trained and guided by professional wildlife biologist Felipe Rodriguez, and Seri field technicians contribute their traditional ecological knowledge of wildlife and their knowledge of plant ecology from their training through NAU's para-ecology training program. The Comcáac team is training other indigenous groups in the region.

Conclusion

These two case studies illustrate different approaches to wild species and habitat protection in native lands. The first case study examines a community-based and biocultural approach to sea turtle conservation in the context of the development of a community-based management plan in El Sargento, a coastal mangrove estuary and fishing camp. The second case study considers a bighorn sheep recovery project on Tiburon Island with significant government involvement. The sea turtle conservation project is nested in a multispecies and habitat management plan that is in development. The bighorn sheep project is a species-specific project on protected lands, with government agreements in place to generate economic benefits to the community.

A comparison of these two different approaches illustrates the benefits and challenges of different strategies to promote the ecological integrity of wildlands and seas and the well-being of their inhabitants in a context that is fraught with complexity. Strategies used for protecting wild species and wildlands on native lands include the following:

- Tribal sovereignty—tribal oversight and management of land and marine territory;

- Collaboration and agreements with government institutions and nongovernmental organizations;
- Recognition of tribal rights to sustainable use of natural resources for their livelihood;
- Education and training in native and Western sciences and culture;
- Community-based management planning process and implementation that includes women and elders;
- Building mutual support networks with other conservation organizations;
- Use of cultural and biological keystone species and conservation flagship species to protect the habitat for multiple species.

Acknowledgments

We gratefully acknowledge the following supporters and collaborators: the Comcáac Government, especially the late Pedro Romero; Mexico's Secretaria del Medio Ambiente y Recursos Naturales, Islas del Golfo; New Mexico Department of Game and Fish; U.S. Fish and Wildlife Service; U.S. Fish and Wildlife Foundation; Overbrook Foundation; The Christensen Fund; David and Lucille Packard Foundation; Propeninsula; World Wildlife Fund; Eahrlam College; American Friends Service Committee; The Foundation for North American Wild Sheep, Sierra Madre; and Northern Arizona University's Center for Sustainable Environments and Department of Applied Indigenous Studies.

References

Excurra E. Bourillon, L. Cantu A. Martinez, M. A., and Alejandro Robles, 2002. "Ecological Conservation" in T. J. Case, M. L. Cody, and E. Ezcurra, *A New Island Biography of the Sea of Cortéz*. New York: Oxford University Press.

Gomex-Pompa, A. yr Dirzo, 1995. Reservas de la biosfera y otras areas naturals protegidasde Mexico. Insitituto Nacional de Estastica and Comision Nacional Para el Conocimiento y Uso de la Biodiversidad.

Meltzer, Lorayne, 2004. "Export Market Influence on the Development of the Pacific Shrimp Fishery of Guaymas, Sonora, Mexico," in the Gulf of California Conference 2004 proceedings. Tucson, Arizona.

Nabhan, G. P., 2000. *Singing the Turtles to Sea: The Comcáac (Seri) Art and Science of Reptiles*. Berkeley: University of California Press.

Chapter 5

~~~~~~~~~~~~~

The Wai Wai
Land Management Model,
Guyana

Cemci Sose (James Suse),
Councilor, Masakenari Village Council,
Kanashen District, Guyana

Location of Kanashen and Masakenari

Kanashen, also known as Konashen (homesteads), is in southern
Guyana. The Kanashen area commences at the mouth of the
Kassikaityu River and stretches from the left bank of the Essequibo
River up the Kassikaityu to its source at the Guyana–Brazil border,
southeast along the border to the watershed of the Essequibo and
New Rivers, north along the watershed to the source of the Amuku
River, along the right bank of the Essequibo, down the Amuku to its
mouth, and then down the Essequibo to the point of origin.
Masakenari (Misakinari), the most remote Amerindian village in
Guyana, is the only inhabited village in Kanashen District, and it is the
seat of the Village Council.

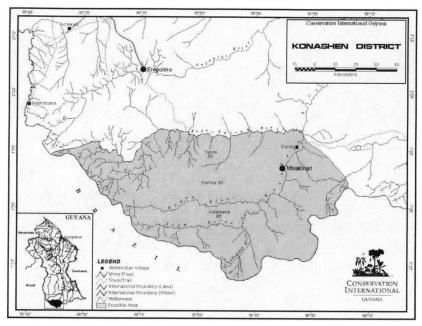

Fig. 5.1. The Kanashen (Konashen) District in southern Guyana

Land Title

For some time, the Wai Wai people petitioned the government for land title. On February 10, 2004, the president of Guyana, His Excellency Bharrat Jagdeo, signed the order to grant the Wai Wai Amerindian Community of Kanashen 625,000 hectares (1.5 million acres) of land. This area is the largest titled to an Amerindian community in Guyana.

Like all other Guyanese, the Wai Wai people do not own subsurface rights. However, they have exclusive rights to the forest resources.

Upon receipt of the land title, the Wai Wai requested Conservation International Guyana (CI-Guyana), through the government of Guyana, to partner with them in managing their lands as a community conservation area (CCA). The Wai Wai, CI-Guyana, and the government signed a memorandum of cooperation to formalize this groundbreaking arrangement. A thorough, transparent, and consultative process among the Wai Wai, the Ministry of Amerindian Affairs, the Environmental Protection Agency, the Regional Democratic Council Region nine, and CI-Guyana preceded attaining the grant.

Land Management

Land is managed through the Konashen Village Council, and the council makes all decisions in consultation with the villagers. A captain, or *toshao*, presides over the council.

CI-Guyana is partnering with the Wai Wai people to develop a management plan for the Wai Wai–owned CCA. Currently, the village captain enforces the village rules, but soon a management plan will be put in place to help enforce those rules.

The entire land area is wild; there are many creeks, mountains, and good flat rocks in the river. The community wants to keep the land wild because it is like a mother to them. They get everything they need from the wild, without spending any money. Things collected from the wild include:

- Medicine to cure illness,
- Raw material to build shelter,
- Wild meat for food, and
- Water for domestic purposes.

Collection of resources follows the traditional Wai Wai value: Our ancestors taught us not to waste and to use only what we need. For example, the bow (leperwood) tree has been important to the Wai Wai for generations. Once we only used this tree for bows for ourselves, but then we started selling it. Now we have to go far away to get bow wood.

We complain about fish because in some areas fish populations are going down. We have recommended to stop fishing each April, because this is the time fish lay their eggs. This is the traditional

Fig. 5.2. Village of Masakenari. Courtesy of the Cemci Sose

practice of the Wai Wai people; they begin fishing again in the dry season, starting in August.

At the moment, there is no logging in Masakenari. The Wai Wai log only when we need materials to put up a building. But in the future, when there is a road to transport logs, we will need to do some logging for our living. At the moment, lack of transportation prevents logging. If we start logging, we must only do so for a short time—perhaps three months—then we must stop and maybe go back in about a year's time. If we do not do this, we will destroy the forest. When someone logs too many trees, the wild animals and birds do not remain where they are. They move very far away from the village, causing the people to have a hard time hunting for the meat they need.

There is no gold in Masakenari. Some people still prospect, but no gold has been found. The Wai Wai themselves do some manual mining and prospecting. But before they do that, they must ask the village captain for permission.

Culture

The Wai Wai culture is still strong. One way we celebrate our culture is with three- to four-day ceremonies at Easter and Christmas. Christmas is the larger of the events. Only Wai Wai people are invited, and usually only the Wai Wai in the village attend.

Benefits

We hope that the land we have is here for generations to come. It is our hope that our children can see what was happening during our time, so that they will know how to manage the land. They will know not to waste fish and to use just what they need, because if they waste, they will destroy all. If our land is wasted, it will not benefit future generations.

The Village Council receives money from various activities, including ecotourism, and the money is given to the council's sub-treasurer, who works with the village to decide what to buy.

Specific Challenges and How They Are Addressed

Permission has to be given to visit the area. The Village Council makes a plan with the villagers and discusses what visitors are planning to do. After everyone agrees, we make another plan on how to deal with the visitors when they arrive.

Once we have reached a decision on accommodations and so forth, we set out the rates to be charged. We choose a guide leader who will accompany visitors and transport them wherever they want.

All decisions are made at a council, including discipline for anyone who breaks village rules and customs.

The council meets to decide how to spend village money. The council abides by the majority decision and decides who to entrust with the money, then sends them to buy what we need.

The council decides on the number of birds or other animals that may be caught or exported. We have a public meeting and decide what amount is right; we can catch any amount so long as it is not wasteful. The council sets limits on how many animals can be caught for sale. If villagers want to catch more than the amount agreed upon in the council, they must get permission from the council.

The Village Council handles requests for scientific research. At first the villagers did not know what was going on when scientists came to do research, and it was not explained to us. Now, however, all requests must go through the council, and the researchers must explain what they are going to do. Researchers are required to pay the village, and they are not allowed to be alone in the forest.

The Wai Wai collaboration with CI-Guyana has resulted in improvements in radio communication, electricity supply through a photovoltaic system, a water distribution system, and other forms of assistance. Other partner organizations such as Canada Fund and the Deutsche Gesellschaft für Technische Zusammenarbeit (GTZ), or German Agency for Technical Cooperation, have provided assistance for economic enterprise development. The Wai Wai have participated in community-based tourism exchange visits to Belize and Surama, a Makushi village in the northern Rupununi, Guyana.

Chapter 6

Conservation Alliances with Amerindian Peoples of the Amazon, Brazil

Stephan Schwartzman, Environmental Defense

Barbara Zimmerman, Conservation International

Editor's Note: This paper was published in *Conservation Biology* 19:3 (June 2005), 721–27 and is reprinted with permission. The Kayapó Indians of the southern Amazon were represented at the 1st Native Lands and Wilderness Council by Megaron Txukarramã, Bep Torim Kayapó, Piu-djo Kayapó, and Francisco Rocha of Fundação Nacional do Indio, who presented the situation of the 30-million-acre Kayapó Reserve.

Ongoing alliances between indigenous peoples and conservation organizations in the Brazilian Amazon have helped achieve the official recognition of approximately 100 million hectares (247 million acres) of indigenous lands. The future of Amazonian indigenous reserves is of strategic importance to the fate of biodiversity in the region. We examined the legislation governing resource use on indigenous lands and summarize the history of the Kayapó people's consolidation of their less than 10-million-hectare (24.7-million-acre) territory.

Like many Amazonian indigenous peoples, the Kayapó have halted the expansion of the agricultural frontier on their lands but allow selective logging and gold mining. Prospects for long-term conservation and sustainability on these lands depend on indigenous peoples' understandings of their resource base and on available economic alternatives. Although forest conservation is not guaranteed by either tenure security or indigenous knowledge, indigenous societies' relatively egalitarian common-property resource management regimes, along with adequate incentives and long-term partnerships with conservation organizations, can achieve this result.

Successful initiatives include Conservation International's long-term project with the A'ukre Kayapó village, incipient large-scale territorial monitoring and control in the Kayapó territory, and the Social-Environmental Institute's (Instituto SocioAmbiental or ISA) fifteen-year partnership with the peoples of the Xingu Indigenous Park, with projects centered on territorial monitoring and control, education, community organization, and economic alternatives. A 2005 agreement on ecological restoration of the Xingu River headwaters between ranchers and private companies, indigenous peoples, and environmentalists, brokered by ISA, marks the emergence of an indigenous and conservation alliance of sufficient cohesiveness and legitimacy to negotiate effectively at a regional scale.

Amerindian territories in the Brazilian Amazon comprise more than 100 million hectares (247 million acres), or approximately 21 percent of the Brazilian Amazon (Instituto SocioAmbital, 2004). The territories reside in 400 legally recognized indigenous lands that are inhabited by some 200,000 people, or about 1 percent of the regional population (Ibid). Twenty-nine territories exceed 1 million hectares (World Conservation Monitoring Centre, 1992). State and federal protected areas comprise about 14 percent of the Amazon, and 2 percent (13 million hectares/32 million acres) of the region consists of protected areas or portions of them that overlap indigenous lands

(Ricardo, 2004). Indigenous lands encompass a much broader range of ecosystem types than all other protected areas combined (Peres and Terborgh, 1995; Fearnside, 2003; Nepstad et al., 2005).

Conservation scientists are increasingly convinced that indigenous territories, given their size and protected status, will be a decisive factor in the ultimate fate of Amazonian ecosystems (Peres and Zimmerman, 2001; Pimm et al., 2001; Fearnside, 2003). Indigenous lands and other protected areas act as the principal barrier to forest cutting and fires along the arc of deforestation—the front line of forest destruction moving north from the south and southeast of the Amazon where approximately 80 percent of deforestation is concentrated (Nepstad et al., 2001; Nepstad et al., 2005). The Kayapó indigenous territories of Pará and Mato Grosso and the Xingu Indigenous Park provide a striking example of this barrier effect and show that the presence of Amerindian peoples has halted an intense wave of deforestation for nearly two decades.

Long-term conservation is not guaranteed by either recognizing Amerindian lands or creating protected areas, but strategies for long-term sustainability differ between the two. Projected new infrastructure investments and agricultural expansion in the Amazon are likely to increase deforestation and pressure on indigenous lands and protected areas alike. These likely threats will require new strategies and new investments to both types of areas if their ecological integrity is to be guaranteed.

Legislation, Resource Use, and Threats to Amerindian Territories

The Constitution of Brazil of 1988 (article 231) assures Amerindian peoples' rights to their own social organization, customs, languages, beliefs, and traditions, and to the lands they have traditionally occupied.

The National Indian Foundation, Fundação Nacional do Indio (FUNAI), is the federal government agency responsible for upholding indigenous policy in Brazil. Although indigenous lands are the property of the federal government, indigenous peoples are accorded permanent occupation and exclusive usufruct rights except for mineral and water rights, which remain under government control. Lands traditionally occupied by indigenous peoples are those "permanently inhabited by them, those used for their productive activities, those indispensable to the environmental resources necessary to their well-being, and those necessary to their physical and cultural reproduction, according to their uses, customs, and traditions (Constituição da Republica Federativa do Brasil, article 231, section 1)."

The legal status of resource extraction on indigenous lands remains ambiguous. Although in 1973 FUNAI managed most of the indigenous societies' relations with the outside world, its guardianship has long since been superseded. Indigenous peoples now deal frequently and directly with loggers, miners, local businesses, nongovernmental organizations (NGOs), the media, and state, federal, and municipal agencies, and are themselves largely responsible for monitoring and control of access to their territory. Resource extraction in indigenous areas is usually conducted on an unregulated basis, if not flagrantly illegally, and there is currently no institutional means to legalize or regulate it. Although indigenous peoples have won legal recognition of their land rights to substantial territories, legal parameters for resource use on their lands remain vague. In the absence of clear rules or standards, indigenous groups have adopted pragmatic approaches that depend on alliances with regional, national, and international actors.

The Kayapó case illustrates how indigenous peoples in the Amazon have won control of substantial territories. The colonization frontier reached Kayapó lands early in the 1980s, and the government became unable to enforce the laws that protect indigenous lands from invasion, encroachment, and resource extraction by third parties. Ranchers, colonists, loggers, gold miners, and illegal land speculators—supported by road construction that promotes frontier expansion—began to flagrantly violate the integrity of Amerindian lands in the southern Pará and Mato Grosso states.

Fig. 6.1. Kayapó survival depends on clean, healthy rivers and forests. Courtesy of Vance G. Martin

In the late 1970s, the Kayapó numbered around 1,300 in seven or eight villages in southern Pará and northern Mato Grosso (Bamberger 1979). The only recognized but then still undemarcated Kayapó land was some 2.8 million hectares (6.9 million acres) surrounding the eastern villages (Centro Ecumênico de Documentação e Informação, 1982). In dramatic confrontations in the 1980s, the Kayapó reinvaded ranches, took hostages, seized river crossings, and expelled thousands of gold miners from their territory. These actions reinvented their warrior tradition as part of a political and public relations campaign that proved effective in winning land struggles. During the late 1980s and 1990s, Kayapó chiefs began to selectively allow mahogany (Swietenia macrophylla King) logging and gold mining concessions in exchange for cash, but they were largely able to prevent outsiders from occupying their lands. Ironically, the illegal logging of mahogany contributed to the persistence of forests in the southeastern Amazon; the Kayapó invested part of the returns in protecting their lands.

Fig. 6.2. A few Kayapó chiefs from twenty-one villages meeting in 2005 to form a coalition to defend their territory against construction of dams, farms, and ranches. Courtesy of Vance G. Martin

The Kayapó now number more than 6,000, and their officially ratified territories cover some 11 million hectares (27 million acres) of continuous forest in Pará and Mato Grosso. For more than twenty years, the Kayapó have almost single-handedly protected their territories from invasion. But the Kayapó lack the resources for surveillance and enforcement to deal with a second wave of deforestation and invasion spreading out from the Cuiabá-Santarém Highway. Most logging in that region is illegal and undertaken without the required management plans (Verissimo et al., 1992, 1995, 2002). Loggers reenter forests several times to remove timber as markets develop, roads improve, and transportation costs decrease. These logged forests become degraded, are prone to fire, become infested with vines and weeds, and lose up to half of their canopy cover (Uhl and Vieira, 1989; Verissimo et al., 1992; Cochrane et al., 1999).

Unlike agriculture, logging and gold mining pose a more insidious threat to Amerindian lands and cultures because these activities do not necessarily result in loss of territory. As a result, Amerindian groups may view these activities as economic opportunity rather than invasion. Although gold mining activity on Kayapó lands tapered off in the 1990s with declining gold prices, mahogany logging continued until international pressure led to government action in 2002. Kayapó lands were once rich in mahogany, the most valuable timber species on Earth, but after more than a decade of uncontrolled logging,

Fig. 6.3. Plumes of smoke drift over the remaining forested areas (dark) of the Kayapó to the north and Parque Indigena do Xingo to the south. This July 2004 MODIS satellite image shows the extent of deforestation (light gray) surrounding the territories of the indigenous peoples.

mahogany is scarce. Inevitably, prices for other timber species will rise in the absence of mahogany as transportation costs decrease with better roads, as regional timber stocks outside Kayapó lands are depleted, and as Kayapó communities are again pressured to sell timber. Although the light intensity of mahogany logging (less than one tree extracted per hectare) did not seriously compromise forest ecology, a higher intensity, multispecies harvest would be permanently damaging (Zimmerman et al., 2001). A 2001 study by the Amazon Institute of People and the Environment (Instituto do Homem e Meio Ambiente da Amazônia, or IMAZON) shows that approximately 25 percent of Kayapó lands in Pará and Mato Grosso are vulnerable to logging of a suite of high-value timber species under the present road network (Lentini et al., 2004).

Conservation of Amerindian Societies and Their Lands

Although necessary, tenure security for indigenous peoples is not tantamount to sustainable management. Typically, indigenous peoples will need new institutions to manage resources (Brandon, 1996). But control of access to resources in a frontier "no man's land" is the sine qua non of any strategy for sustainability in large tropical landscapes, and Amerindian peoples have largely achieved this thus far (Instituto SocioAmbiental, 2004). The conservation issue in the Amazon needs to be addressed next.

Amerindians in the Amazon generally see animals, plants, rivers, and forests as the basis for reproduction of their societies, although they may have no cultural restriction against resource extraction—at times to the point of exhaustion of a particular resource (Turner, 2000). Conservationists have sometimes oversimplified traditional knowledge and resource management as benign conservation strategies, and externally induced change as detrimental to sustainable practices (Brandon, 1996; Berkes, 2004).

Social and cultural change may not always compromise long-term sustainability. However, what is considered traditional knowledge may be neither traditional in the sense of ancient and unchanging, nor necessarily beneficial for the resource base. Both traditional indigenous institutions and recent social and cultural innovations have at times enabled environmental gains and at other times have jeopardized the sustainability of the currently protected territories.

For example, Kayapó social organization was characterized recently by intense, often violent factionalism and competition based on leadership in warfare (Verswijver, 1992). The wide geographic distribution of Kayapó villages in the 1970s—the basis for subsequent successful land claims—is largely a result of this process. But rivalry among headmen, derived from warfare and ritual wealth, led to internal competition for logging and mining deals and the apparent windfall of goods they provided. For the Xicrin Kayapó people, the historical process of contact with frontier society, which began in the early decades of the twentieth century, was driven at least as much by Xicrin strategies to access the wealth of outsiders for their own social and cultural motivations as it was by an externally induced process (Gordon, 2003). In the Xingu Park, in contrast, traditional knowledge has preserved a wealth of indigenous cultigens while impeding the assimilation of the concept of finite natural resources (Ricardo, 2001). In sum, traditional or indigenous knowledge may be more hybrid and less static than is often recognized, and more dynamic and adaptive than indigenous peoples' own representations may lead us to believe (Dove, 2002; Schwartzman, 2005).

Amerindian societies do nevertheless generally conform to the criteria that sociologists have identified as requisite for successful common-property resource management regimes (Ostrom, 1990; Becker and Ostrom, 1995; Morrow and Hull, 1996; Gibson et al., 2000):

- Clear definition of the resource and its users and the ability of users to sustain legal claims to or effectively defend the resource from outsiders;
- Clear criteria for membership as an eligible user;
- Rapid access to low-cost, internally adaptive mechanisms of conflict resolution;
- Fair decision-making rights and use rights among users, as in egalitarian Amerindian society;
- No challenge to or undermining of institutions created and defined by users by any other authorities; and,

- User communities accustomed to negotiating and cooperating with each other.

Although Amerindian societies possess these attributes associated with successful common-property regimes, development and predatory resource exploitation from outside will exert high levels of pressure. For the long-term preservation of forest ecosystems, Amerindians need economic alternatives—congruent with their cultural norms—that they can control. Conservation and development projects with Amerindian communities must therefore be designed around normative aboriginal values of equity, cooperation, and reciprocity that are expressed in terms of local authority achieved by consensus and common-property access, rather than relying on western normative values of competition, exclusive rights to resources, and centralized management authority (Chapeskie, 1995).

Examples of Conservation Alliances with Amerindian Societies

Kayapó and Conservation International

The Kayapó have drawn on their social institutions and collective organization to forge their own forms of resistance and accommodation to Brazilian society. Unlike other politically active Amazonian groups, they have neither joined nor cooperated with any interethnic organization. Historically, Kayapó leadership was validated by securing resources from beyond the village boundaries, such as leading long hunting treks or raiding the villages of other Kayapó or Brazilians.

With contact, the requisites of leadership changed. Fluency in Portuguese, basic literacy, arithmetic skills, and familiarity with Brazilian administrative and economic institutions became essential assets. During the years of mahogany logging that introduced foreign concepts to the Kayapó society, the collective organization of Kayapó communities remained strong. In several villages that had allowed extraction of mahogany and gold, communal control was eventually asserted over the younger leaders who had parlayed their skills as intercultural mediators into political and economic dominance in the community. This control meant either that communities stopped extraction activities altogether on their land or made their leaders share the profits.

Conservation International do Brasil (CI–Brasil) began working with a single Kayapó community, A'Ukre, in 1992, with the objective of giving this community an economic alternative to selling mahogany logs. The A'Ukre conservation enterprise is an ecological research station and biological reserve that attracts researchers because it is ecologically intact with a full complement of timber tree species. The site is protected from logging and hunting and is embedded within a much larger wilderness area, itself protected from deforestation. Ecological research generates direct benefits for the community in the form of user fees for communal use, employment, training, and administrative and technical support in the outside world. Recognizing the benefits from their growing research station enterprise, this community chose to maintain an 8,000-hectare (19,800-acre) mahogany and ecological research reserve in lieu of continuing to sell mahogany for short-term gain (Zimmerman et al., 2001).

Once gold mining and mahogany logging on Kayapó lands were interrupted, the Kayapó began organizing associations to access support for community needs. CI-Brasil provides substantial technical, administrative, and financial support and related project implementation needs for the two main Kayapó NGOs: Associação Floresta Protegida (AFP) in Pará state and Instituto Raoní (IR) of Mato Grosso state. Both organizations are implementing territorial surveillance and conservation and development projects (research station, Brazil nut extraction, and *piqui* fruit harvest, among others) with funding obtained principally by CI–Brasil and in partnership with FUNAI. The FUNAI does not have nearly enough resources to uphold its constitutional obligation of protecting indigenous peoples and their lands. NGOs can help fill this gap under the partnership model used by the AFP and by the IR.

The role of the AFP, IR, and FUNAI is to support Kayapó surveillance and development initiatives as long as they act to preserve social and environmental integrity. The AFP, IR, Kayapó leaders, and FUNAI design and help coordinate surveillance strategies among guard posts and communities; the AFP and IR support administration, infrastructure, and training for implementing the strategy; the Kayapó perform ground surveillance and occupation of their territory; and FUNAI provides legal authority, coordination, and administration of field activities and involvement of other federal authorities.

In addition to ongoing support for the local Kayapó NGOs, CI–Brasil provides the means for Kayapó leadership, dispersed across a vast expense of territory, to meet annually. These meetings serve as a collective forum to achieve consensus, an important principle of Kayapó society, and to unite leadership and reinforce traditional Kayapó political institutions. Fortified by their institutions, the Kayapó have

Fig. 6.4. A young Kayapó girl, Kendjan Village. Courtesy of Vance G. Martin

been among the strongest and most politically successful defenders of indigenous rights of all peoples of the Brazilian Amazon.

Xingu Indigenous Park and Instituto SocioAmbiental

Unlike the Kayapó, the various societies in the Xingu Indigenous Park have not permitted logging or gold mining on their territory. The Xingu Park, about 2.6 million hectares (6.4 million acres) in northern Mato Grosso, was created in 1961, largely through the efforts of renowned indigenists the Villas Boas brothers. This area is now inhabited by some 3,700 people of sixteen distinct ethnicities and has been continuously inhabited for at least 800 years (Heckenberger et al., 2003). The Xingu tribes (Xinguanos) have repeatedly turned back illegal loggers, held and seized the equipment of intruders hunting and fishing in the park, and defended the boundaries of the area from surrounding ranchers throughout the 1980s and 1990s, despite expansion of the agricultural frontier around the park. The Villas Boas implemented a paternalistic system (continued by FUNAI), whereby chiefs' allegiance to park authorities was ensured by giving them trade goods. As the Indians' need for outside goods grew, this gift system collapsed and opportunities to generate income, outside of a handful of FUNAI jobs and the sale of handicrafts and artwork, were extremely limited.

In the 1980s, it was also becoming clear that the original design of the park, leaving the headwaters of the major tributaries of the Xingu River unprotected, was flawed. Water quality began to deteriorate, with increased siltation and turbidity (Ricardo, 2001). Starting in 1990, one of Brazil's principal indigenous rights and environmental organizations, the ISA, set up a project in the Xingu Park and helped the Xingu peoples organize the Xingu Lands Indigenous Association, Associção das Terras Indigenas de Xingu, or ATIX, in an effort to achieve greater political and economic autonomy. The ISA and ATIX undertook a territorial monitoring and control project, building and manning control posts, patrolling borders, and maintaining the demarcation of park boundaries. The ISA further obtained support for and instituted a bilingual education program, concentrating on the training of indigenous teachers and, with ATIX, mapping resource use and studying economic alternatives.

The fact that the Xingu groups did not permit logging or gold mining on their territory may in part result from the absence of mahogany in the area, but also undoubtedly owes to ISA's long-term partnership and investments in economic alternatives. After a decade of dialogue, research, and pilot initiatives, twenty-eight villages in the northern and middle Xingu are producing certified organic honey. The ATIX cooperative has a contract with one of Brazil's largest supermarket chains, which currently buys the entire output.

The ISA–ATIX partnership has developed into an important example of frontier governance (Nepstad et al., 2002). In 2003, the organizations conducted a field survey of environmental conditions of the upper headwaters of the Xingu and found that about one-third of the original vegetation cover had been cleared. They identified soil erosion and water supply as major problems within and outside the park. Ranchers, soybean farmers, and colonists had, to varying degrees, ignored stipulations of the forestry code requiring each property to maintain 20 percent of its original forest cover, especially along rivers and streams.

The team found ample evidence of pesticide pollution of watercourses. Based on this survey, ISA organized a series of meetings with local landowners, businesses, ranchers' unions, and state and federal producer's organizations, including the powerful National Confederation of Agriculture, to seek avenues for dialogue on addressing environmental degradation of the headwaters.

Staff from ISA identified the restoration and protection of riparian forest as one issue on which dialogue was feasible and organized a meeting of ranchers, businesses, colonists, environmentalists, and indigenous peoples in Canarana, Mato Grosso, in 2004. Participants reached an unprecedented agreement in favor of restoring and protecting riparian forests. In essence, ranchers, soy producers, environmentalists, and indigenous peoples agreed to seek subsidized official credit for landowners to restore and protect riparian forest in the Xingu headwaters. The novelty of this meeting was the emergence of sufficiently organized and representative stakeholders to allow a negotiation capable of changing regional processes.

Conclusion

Both the Kayapó and Xinguanos emerged in the 1980s and 1990s as cohesive regional actors with significant effects on the extent and direction of frontier expansion in places of great conservation value. The Xinguanos' defense of their territory and the Kayapó's successful reincorporation of a large part of their undemarcated lands resulted in a continuous north–south corridor of some 14 million hectares (35 million acres) of protected forest.

Social and cultural changes in the Xingu and among the Kayapó have demonstrably resulted in increased pressure on natural resources and losses of traditional knowledge. But they have also resulted in dynamic new strategies with enormous positive conservation value. The innovative negotiation brokered by ISA and ATIX with regional and national agribusiness promises to achieve a precedent-setting, regional resource management process. Although it could be said that the Xingu groups have adopted a more sustainable resource use strategy than the Kayapó, the same aggressive independence and warrior tradition that led the Kayapó to broker their own deals with regional economic interests also motivated their strategy of territorial consolidation. Their profits from logging and mining partially funded these gains and the protection of their territory. The Kayapó's financial independence, costly though it has been in terms of resources lost to the communities, enabled the group to make critical interventions in key moments for national policy, such as the Constituent Assembly of 1988. What may prove most important to conservationists is that in relation to outsiders, both Kayapó and Xinguanos are organized and cohesive enough that with adequate support they can control access to their lands and negotiate with other social and economic actors on a regional scale.

Conservation NGOs can make the most of ample Amerindian knowledge, their experience of frontier expansion, and successful common property regimes, to forge further wide-reaching, long-term alliances with tribes for the conservation of Amazonian ecosystems. Investments in territorial control and economic alternatives for Amerindian peoples form the basis of long-term conservationist and indigenous alliances that can affect frontier expansion and forest protection at a significant scale. The challenge is to devise long-term investment strategies that remunerate indigenous peoples for the ecosystem services of the lands they protect, directly linking development benefits with conservation.

References

Bamberger, J., 1979. Exit and voice in central Brazil: the politics of flight in Kayapó society. Pages 129–146 in D. Maybury-Lewis, editor. *Dialectical societies: the Ge and Bororó of Central Brazil.* Harvard University Press, Cambridge, Massachusetts.

Becker, D., and E. Ostrom, 1995. Human ecology and resource sustainability: the importance of institutional diversity. *Annual Review of Ecology and Systematics* 26: 113–133.

Chapter 7

~~~~~~~~~~

Land Use Planning and Community-Based Natural Resource Management in Kokolopori, The Democratic Republic of Congo

Albert Lokasola,

President, Vie Sauvage,

Kokolopori, The Democratic Republic of Congo

Michael Hurley,

Executive Director, Bonobo Conservation Initiative,

Washington, DC

Kokolopori is located within Equatuer Province in the Cuvette Centrale of the Democratic Republic of Congo (DRC). The Kokolopori Bonobo Reserve, a community-based reserve (CBR) covers approximately 186,000 hectares (460,000 acres). The reserve area encompasses forests that have been historically recognized as traditional lands of the Mongandu people and is made up primarily of old growth and secondary growth forests. The villages and agricultural areas are situated mainly along a single seventy-one-kilometer (forty-four-mile) long road, leaving large undisturbed forest blocs with rich biodiversity.

Berkes, F., 2004. Rethinking community-based conservation. *Conservation Biology* 18: 621–630.

Brandon, K., 1996. Traditional peoples, nontraditional times: social change and the implications for biodiversity conservation. Pages 219–236 in K. Redford and J. Mansour, editors. *Traditional peoples and biodiversity conservation in large tropical landscapes*. The Nature Conservancy, Arlington, Virginia.

Centro Ecumênico de Documentação e Informação (CEDI), 1982. Povos indígenas no Brasil/1981. CEDI, São Paulo (in Portuguese).

Chapeskie, A., 1995. Land, landscape, culturescape: aboriginal relationships to land and the co-management of natural resources. Report for the Royal Commission on Aboriginal Peoples, Land, Resource and Environment Regimes Project. The Government of Canada, Department of Indian and Northern Affairs, Quebec.

Cochrane M. A., A. Alencar, M. D. Schulze, C. M. Souza Jr., D. C. Nepstad, P. Lefebvre, and E. A. Davidson, 1999. Positive feedbacks in the fire dynamics of closed-canopy tropical forests. *Science* 284: 1832–1835.

Dove, M., 2002. Hybrid histories and indigenous knowledge among Asian rubber smallholders. *International Social Science Journal* 173: 349–359.

Fearnside, P. M., 2003. Conservation policy in Brazilian Amazonia: understanding the dilemmas. *World Development* 31: 757–779.

Gibson, C. C., M. A. McKean, and E. Ostrom, editors, 2000. *People and forests: communities, institutions, and governance*. The MIT Press, Cambridge, Massachusetts.

Gordon, C., 2003. Folhas pálidas: a incorporação Xikrin (Mebêngôkre) do dinheiro e das mercadorias. PhD thesis. Museu Nacional, Universidade Federal do Rio de Janeiro, Rio de Janeiro (in Portuguese).

Heckenberger, M., A. Kuikuro, U. T. Kuikuro, J. C. Russel, M. Schmidt, C. Fausto, and B. Franchetto, 2003. Amazonia 1492: pristine forest or cultural parkland? *Science* 301: 1710–1713.

Instituto SocioAmbiental (ISA), 2004. Amazônia Brasileira 2004. ISA, São Paulo (in Portuguese).

Lentini, M., R. Salomão, C. Souza Jr., G. Gomes, and P. Amaral, 2004. Análise da pressão madeireira nas Terras Indigenas do sul do estado do Pará. Relatório Técnico, Conservation International do Brasil, Belém, Brasil (in Portuguese).

Laurance, W. F., A. K. M. Albernaz, P. M. Fearnside, H. Vasconcelos, and L. V. Ferreira, 2004. Deforestation in Amazonia. *Science* 304: 1109–1111.

Morrow, C. E., and R. W. Hull, 1996. Donor-initiated common pool resource institutions: the case of the Yanesha forestry cooperative. *World Development* 24: 1641–1657.

Nepstad, D., et al., 2001. Road paving, fire regime feedbacks, and the future of Amazon forests. *Forest Ecology and Management* 154: 395–407.

Nepstad, D., D. McGrath, A. Alencar, A. C. Barros, G. Carvalho, M. Santilli, and M. del C. Vera Diaz, 2002. Frontier governance in Amazonia. *Science* 295: 629–631.

Nepstad, D., S. Schwartzman, B. Bamberger, M. Santilli, D. Ray, P. Schlesinger, P. Lefebvre, A. Alencar, and E. Prinz, 2005. Inhibition of Amazon deforestation and fire by parks and Indigenous reserves. *Conservation Biology* 20: 65–73.

Ostrom, E., 1990. *Governing the commons: the evolution of institutions for collective action*. Cambridge University Press, Cambridge, United Kingdom.

Peres, C. A., 1994. Indigenous reserves and nature conservation in Amazonian forests. *Conservation Biology* 8: 586–588.

Peres, C. A., and J. W. Terborgh, 1995. Amazonian nature reserves: an analysis of the defensibility status of existing conservation units and design criteria for the future. *Conservation Biology* 9: 34–46.

Peres, C. A., and B. L. Zimmerman, 2001. Perils in parks or parks in peril: reconciling conservation in Amazonian reserves with and without use. *Conservation Biology* 15: 793–797.

Pimm, S. L., et al., 2001. Can we defy nature's end? *Science* 293: 2207–2208.

Ricardo, C. A., 2001. Povos indígenas no Brasil 1996/2000. Instituto SocioAmbiental, São Paulo (in Portuguese).

Schwartzman, S., 2005. Nature and culture in central Brazil: Pana resource concepts. *Journal of Sustainable Forestry*: in pre

Turner, T., 2000. Indigenous rights, environmental protectior struggle over forest resources in the Amazon: the ca Brazilian Kayapó. Pages 226–261 in J. Conway, K. Kenist Marx, editors. *Earth, air, fire and water: the humanities an ronment*. University of Massachusetts Press, Amherst.

Uhl, C., and I. C. Vieira, 1989. Ecological impacts of selective loggi Brazilian Amazon: a case study from the Paragominas r the state of Para. *Biotropica* 21: 98–106.

Veríssimo, A., P. Barreto, M. Mattos, R. Tarifa, and C. Uhl, 1992. impacts and prospects for sustainable forest manageme old Amazonian frontier: the case of paragominas. *Forest and Management* 55: 169–199.

Verswijver, G., 1992. The club fighters of the Amazon: warfare am Kaiapó Indians of central Brazil. Rijksuniversiteit Gent, Ge Netherlands.

Veríssimo, A., P. Barreto, R. Tarifa, and C. Uhl, 1995. Extraction of value natural resource from Amazonia: the case of mah *Forest Ecology and Management* 72: 39–60.

Veríssimo, A., M. A. Cochrane, C. Souza Jr., and R. Salomão, 2002. P areas for establishing national forests in the Brazilian An *Conservation Ecology* 6: 4.

World Conservation Monitoring Centre (WCMC), 1992. Protected ar the world: a review of national systems. Volume 4. Nearcti Neotropical. WCMC, Cambridge, United Kingdom.

Zimmerman, B. L., C. A. Peres, J. R. Malcolm, and T. Turner, Conservation and development alliances with the Kayap south-eastern Amazonia, a tropical forest indigenous pe *Environmental Conservation* 28: 8–22.

Kokolopori forest is a community forest under the new DRC forestry code classification; the CBR will be designated as a Reserves Naturelle under the forestry code, encompassing a core area of highest biodiversity protection, surrounded by multiuse zones, and managed by the local people.

Kokolopori is surrounded by an area of expanding agriculture and plantations. Pushed by economic collapse, political instability, and armed conflicts, export farming companies have retreated from the region since 1970, and the agro-industrial pressure that tends to convert large-scale forests to plantations is low. Among the sixty logging companies operating or allowed to operate in Equateur Province where the Kokolopori forest is located, none of them operates inside Kokolopori.

Another key factor affecting planning is the recent war's devastation of infrastructure throughout the region. This affects all

Fig. 7.1. Bais, or forest clearings, such at this one at Yotemankele, are just one of the many habitats found in the Kokoklopori area. Large mammals such as bongos and sitatungs vist them. Courtesy of Michael Hurley, Bonobo Conservation Initiative

aspects of society, including communications; transportation; access to goods, services, and capital; education; and health care. The country's health care system has nearly collapsed, ranking 179 out of 191 countries surveyed by the World Health Organization.

In 2001, Medécins Sans Frontières (MSF) conducted a survey in the region to assess mortality, access to health care, vaccination coverage, and exposure to violence. High mortality rates were found, mainly due to malnutrition and infectious diseases. Approximately 10 percent of the total population and 25 percent of the population under the age of five had perished in the year before the survey. Most people in Kokolopori have no access to any formal health care. Although we recognize the importance of promoting an integration of traditional healing systems as well as protecting indigenous peoples' rights and their royalties from potential pharmaceutical products derived from the local rainforest, it is critical that access to basic health care be incorporated into programs developed in cooperation with international partners.

Current conservation activities in Kokolopori include:

- Infrastructure improvement;
- Monitoring of nine semihabituated bonobo groups in three stations that employ twenty-one crew members and control some 12,000 hectares (30,000 acres) of land;
- Completion of large mammal surveys and mapping the flagship species distribution to assess the overall potential of the forest;
- Preparation of the zoning exercise that should result in the creation of core conservation zones, buffers, and multiple-use zones;
- Education programs including the establishment of the Institute Superieur de Developmente Rurale, a technical

college that will provide training in sustainable agriculture, micro-enterprise management, and a sensitization campaign; and,

- Reserve development that works to strengthen the local bonobo reserve association and to build capacities for sustainable farming, micro-enterprise, and local development through micro-credit.

Kokolopori falls within the Maringa/Lopori-Wamba Forest landscape, designated as an area of high-priority protection by the newly inaugurated Congo Basin Forest Partnership (CBFP), a consortium of international conservation organizations funded through a variety of mechanisms including the Central African Regional Program for the Environment (CARPE/USAID). One of the current challenges and opportunities is to coordinate planning and acquire appropriate funding through this mechanism, as well as to assure that the rights and interests of the local indigenous people are addressed.

Biodiversity Conservation

Although there are number of important considerations in the development of land use plans, I begin with discussions regarding biodiversity conservation in Kokolopori, as we have a unique opportunity upon which to build: the conservation of a flagship species, bonobos.

One of the most critical aspects of this endeavor, which not only highlights an urgent need, but also highlights challenges and opportunities, is protecting bonobos. Bonobos (*Pan paniscus*) are one of only four great ape species. Bonobos share approximately 99 percent of their DNA with humans; however, they are the least known and least protected great ape. Known especially for their cooperative and matriarchal society, bonobos only live in the Cuvette Centrale of the DRC. Recent war

Fig. 7.2. Bonobos, Kokolopori's flagship species. Copyright
Jeffrey Oonk

and infrastructure breakdown—which has killed more than 3 million
people since 1998—also appears to have had a devastating impact on
bonobo populations. There have been estimates of 5,000 to 10,000 left
in the wild, but there are no current accurate estimates.

The extinction of bonobos would be a tremendous tragedy.
Bonobos shed a distinctive light on primate evolution. Unlike the more
widely known chimpanzee, whose male-dominated society is marked
by power politics and aggression, bonobos live in a society characterized by sharing and cooperation and a creative use of sex to resolve
conflicts and promote harmony. The bonobo is also a unique and
distinctive flagship species. We can use the bonobo to promote awareness of its rainforest habitat and to act as a symbol the Congolese can
look to to represent peace and sharing, concepts greatly needed in the
war-torn Congo, where conflict is driven by uncontrolled exploitation
of resources.

The land use planning process implemented in Kokolopori
builds greatly upon the protection of the bonobo and other important
species. While this model cannot necessarily be applied to all

programs of indigenous land use planning, throughout the world many places that still have vast tracts of wilderness and rich biodiversity are the places where indigenous people still have some control of their land and resources. The protection of these forests is often due to indigenous belief systems that emphasize living in harmony with the environment and have promoted spiritual bonds with nature.

Fig. 7.3. Line transect methodology training. Courtesy of Albert Lokasola, Vie Sauvage

From a land use planning perspective, there are a number of practical applications of the flagship species concept.

1. The opportunity to attract international attention and funding. This is a prime consideration in the development of the Kokolopori Bonobo Reserve. Vie Sauvage has partnered with the Bonobo Conservation Initiative, which has provided funding, training, and capacity building, and has helped attract other international organizations/investors, including the U.S. Fish & Wildlife Service's Great Ape Conservation Fund, Conservation International, The Global Conservation Fund, and the South East Consortium for International Development. Conservation organizations are often the first to arrive in remote regions such as Kokolopori to provide support. Our challenge is to build

upon their initial support to address other social and economic needs.

2. The opportunity to support and build on local belief systems. In Kokolopori, the Mongandu people have spiritual and historic bonds with bonobos. Bonobos are recognized as relatives, and the local folkloric tradition has many stories of the importance of bonobo–human interaction. There are taboos against killing bonobos. The funding and support for bonobo protection that international organizations provide validates indigenous belief systems. Throughout the world, indigenous cultures are being assimilated into modern societies; indigenous youth are often drawn to civilization and a desire to cast off and lose respect for their historic traditions. The interest and funding provided by international organizations helps strengthen and rebuild respect for local traditions.

Fig 7.4. Representatives from twenty-four Kokolopori villages honor Vie Sauvage leader Leonard, seated, for his work protecting bonobos at an annual ritual. Courtesy of Michael Hurley, Bonobo Conservation Initiative

3. Mapping and land use planning. The identification of flagship species ranges and other important biodiversity indicators provide a basis to map and establish core protected areas, buffer zones, corridors, and agricultural areas. In contrast with some historic designations of parks and protected areas, the local people of Kokolopori are full participants in determining these zones, and the zoning is built upon their historic beliefs.

Government Policies

Three key governmental and legislative elements affect the development of a land use management plan: the new DRC Code Foresterie (Forest Code), the Droit de Foncier, and traditional and current political systems.

The new Code Foresterie (Law No. 011-2002) provides that protected areas are to cover 15 percent of the national territory. It introduces innovations in DRC including:

- mandatory implementation of forest management plans;
- public auctioning of forest concessions with the distribution of 40 percent of the resulting receipts to decentralized entities;
- rights for local communities to directly manage their own forest concessions; and,
- the establishment of Forest Consultative Councils at national and provincial levels.

The code sets principles, but detailed regulations still need to be defined. The DRC's new Forest Code primarily covers development related to forestry and logging concessions. However, specific regulations are necessary to enforce these rights effectively.

The code theoretically takes into account the customary rights of local communities with regard to any concession contract with logging companies, as well as consultation with local communities as a mandatory step for all procedures leading to the designation of forest areas. However, there are still a number of concerns regarding its potential implementation, and there are indigenous groups in the DRC who have raised serious issues including:

- The management of these forests must under no account by guided by the hypothesis that the development of industrial forest activity necessarily contributes to the development of the people, nor of its most disadvantaged sectors.

- The code takes insufficient account of the specific needs of forest-dependent communities and could lead to serious conflicts over community rights and access to forest resources.

To quote Aldo Leopold, often credited as the "founding father of wildlife ecology": "Having to squeeze the last drop of utility out of the land has the same desperate finality as having to chop up the furniture to keep warm."

The Droit de Foncier, as opposed to the Forest Code, which mainly covers forestry and logging concession rights, relates to land tenure and land use rights of local populations. These rights vary from region to region but often incorporate historic traditional systems respecting the local chieftainships and tribal systems. Building upon this system, it is possible to establish specific rights for the local population under a participatory land use management plan for Kokolopori.

Throughout the DRC, as elsewhere in the world, traditional and tribal systems have been affected by colonial powers; national and local political systems have been imposed. It is fortunate that in DRC, these systems were often built upon the existing hierarchical systems.

For example, in Equateur there is a provincial authority, the governor, a district administrator in Tshuapa, and a territorial administrator in Djolu. These are DRC government-sanctioned authorities. These authorities recognize the political and traditional power of the local chiefdoms, whose chiefs have real authority. In Kokolopori there are four *groupementes*, each with its own chief. Groupementes are made up of five or six villages, with village chiefs having village authority.

In Kokolopori, the people are bound by a spiritual and religious tradition that enhances the authority of the chiefs and allows for cohesive planning and management. The Kokolopori Bonobo Reserve Association (KBRA) has been formed to manage and develop the reserve, and is made up of all groupement and village chiefs. Decisions are made on a participatory basis.

Fig. 7.5. Conservation and sustainable development programs build upon and show respect for traditional beliefs and political structures. Here community members participate in a KBRA spiritual gathering and community awareness raising program. Courtesy of Michael Hurley, Bonobo Conservation Initiative

Land Use Planning and Management

Success in establishing the Kokolopori Bonobo Reserve results in part from an information exchange program developed by Vie Sauvage and the Bonobo Conservation Initiative.

Throughout the Congo, people have proven to be remarkable managers of their natural resources, despite decades of overwhelming political and economic constraints. Indigenous local knowledge consequently has a crucial role to play in preserving the vast natural heritage of the Congo. The information exchange program assesses the knowledge, attitudes, beliefs, and practices (KABP) of indigenous populations, and works toward building constituencies and local partnerships for conservation programs. This information is incorporated into our sensitization and educational outreach campaign to promote a conservation ethic and consensus-building in the region.

The information exchange program supports a two-way flow of information between locals and visiting conservationists, whether Congolese or non-Congolese. A vigorous hybrid of local and imported concepts and practices is less likely to be ignored or resisted than the narrower and didactic approach of instructing local populations without first taking into account what they might know or be able to contribute to species conservation.The information exchange program combines both quantitative and qualitative methods. A preliminary survey of human population distribution includes simple questionnaires designed to elicit information on knowledge, attitudes, beliefs and practices. Of particular interest are hunting practices and ideologies relevant to bonobo conservtion.

Socioeconomic surveys measure human demographics, economic indicators, and land use. Where local practices and ideas clearly work in favor of the preservation of the bonobo and the forest, such as traditional proscriptions on hunting bonobo among Kokolopori and Wamba area populations, they are recorded and disseminated throughout the bonobo habitat. Likewise, particular conservation problems and solutions will be addressed in ongoing activities.

We are blending sacred knowledge and modern science and combining data from GIS systems and biodiversity surveys with indigenous knowledge. For example, in Kokolopori there are specific locations that have historical designations as sacred forests; these are plotted, mapped, and incorporated into land use plans.

Fig. 7.6. A Yetee village chief prepares a ritual to approve further research and entry into the sacred forest. Courtesy of Michael Hurley, Bonobo Conservation Initiative

It is important to note that the surveys and information exchange program have been implemented by Vie Sauvage teams, which are made up of the local indigenous people. Training, equipment, and funding have been provided to ensure survey methodology complies with international standards. The extent of local participation is unusual and has led to more robust results and greater motivation of and participation by the local population.

Many large mammals and other important species have been identified including bongo, forest buffalo, golden cat, leopard, Congo peacock, salongo monkey (which may only exist in Kokolopori), Tshuapa red colobus, and at least eight other primate species. We have geo-referenced core habitats and ranges for a number of species.

Fig. 7.7. A number of tree frog species are common in Kokolopori. Courtesy of Michael Hurley, Bonobo Conservation Initiative

Buffer zones, corridors, and potential multiple-use zones are being identified and mapped, including core conservation areas, agricultural areas, villages, roads, trails, and river access. Anthropogenic and land use information is being compiled. Several key areas have been identified where there are higher threats from hunting and forest clearing for agricultural use.

Analysis of potential nontimber forest products, agricultural and enterprise opportunities, pilot micro-credit, and sustainable agriculture programs have been initiated.

One example of a sustainable development project is the implementation of a mosaic disease-resistant cassava project. Mosaic disease has traditionally wiped out up to 80 percent of cassava production, a staple crop. This has led to expanding fields into primary forests. The introduction of the new crop along with training in sound agricultural practices reduces deforestation and increases food crop, as well as excess for potential sale, thus generating revenues for the local population.

In response to international investment in conservation efforts that include communications, transport, training and capacity building (high-frequency radio, motorcycles, fuel, equipment, and so forth), the community has made investments in building conservation and education centers, and made commitments to improve roads, and the like.

As previously stated, villages and agricultural fields line the single main road through Kokolopori. This traditional structure is comparable to the modern concept of cluster dwelling, where large sections of the natural landscape remain intact and human activities are concentrated. This traditional system has protected the forest and its species and has attracted international support and cooperation.

Community-based organizations have also been established in affiliation with the Kokolopori Reserve Association, including the Cooperatif Agricultural de L'Est de La Cuvette (CAPEC) and the Kokolopori Women's Association. These groups are taking the lead in implementing agricultural and micro-credit programs.

Fig. 7.8. A newly built Vie Sauvage and Kokolopori Bonobo Reserve Association (KBRA) Conservation and Education Center. Conservation centers such as this have been started in three key villages. Courtesy of Bienvenu Mupenda

Fig. 7.9. Soap making training sponsored by the Kokolopori
Women's Association. Courtesy of Michael Hurley, Bonobo
Conservation Initiative

Conclusion and Recommendations

One of the real strengths of the Kokolopori Bonobo Reserve is the
power of the Kokolopori Bonobo Reserve Association (KBRA). The
KBRA structure and hierarchy parallels historic tribal political structure
and is made up of tribal leaders and other community members. This
hierarchy is vertically integrated, and because it reflects the traditional
local political hierarchy, it also has formal and official political status on
a regional and territorial basis. Although the KBRA relies heavily on Vie
Sauvage and the Bonobo Conservation Initiative for interim management, funding, and capacity building, it is the KBRA that makes
decisions and approves project implementation.

Conservation, development, and conflict resolution decisions
are still made based on traditional tribal systems with input and support
from outside entities and partners. There is still a great deal of work to
be done as programs are implemented and compromises must be made.
For example, many people in Kokolopori still hunt to provide basic nour-
ishment for their families. We cannot simply impose a ban on hunting;

however we can promote a return to ancient, more sustainable hunting practices such as seasonal and geographic rotation, as well as outright bans in core areas and for certain species. We can also educate the local people about the benefits of maintaining strong populations of certain endangered species. However, the ultimate decisions regarding specific mechanisms and program implementation will come from the KBRA.

The success thus far of the Kokolopori Bonobo Reserve has led to increased external cooperation, which includes attracting additional funding from conservation and development sources. Kokolopori is established as the core pilot program for the Bonobo Peace Forest, a linked constellation of community-based reserves, surrounded by areas of sustainable development that were developed in cooperation with the Bonobo Conservation Initiative and other international and Congolese organizations. Other regional groups have recognized the benefit of this model and have sought regional cooperation. This includes the establishment of the Lonua and Mompano Bonobo Reserves, additionally adding more than 300,000 hectares (741,000 acres) to the Bonobo Peace Forest. These reserves have been initiated through local motivation.

In addition, the Kokolopori Bonobo Reserve Association will work cooperatively with regional plantations to develop sustainable green agricultural development opportunities, which can help develop much-needed revenues for the region in cooperation with international entities interested in conservation.

In conclusion, I offer the following conservation recommendations based on the experience at Kokolopori:

- Develop programs that incorporate flagship species and biodiversity to enhance international investment and partnership opportunities.
- Support and build upon traditional belief systems and indigenous political structures to enhance efficiency. Local

populations must be truly empowered to control their own destiny.

• International cooperation is critical for support. It is extremely important to find international partners who truly support local capacity building and are responsive to the priority needs of the local population.

• It is important to concurrently work at the local, regional, and national levels to assure devolution of authority to local levels.

• Although we have been successful up to a point in Kokolopori, it is still a struggle to assure that as international funding becomes available, an appropriate share of funding is allocated to local populations to support their needs. Forums such as the Wilderness Congress can help assure that guidelines and recommendations are established to promote greater local and indigenous participation in funding and decision making.

7.10. A management training session sponsored by Vie Sauvage for the Women's Association and Cooperatif Agricultural de L'Est de La Cuvette (CAPEC). Management training, as well as conservation and sustainable development training, are important aspects of the program. Courtesy of Michael Hurley, Bonobo Conservation Initiative

Chapter 8

The Tchuma Tchato Community Adopts a Biosphere Approach to African Wilderness, Mozambique

Luís dos Santos Namanha, Chadifira Mussorowanhati, and **Feriado Damião Alferes,**
Tchuma Tchato,
Tete, Mozambique

Sally Wynn and **Duncan Purchase,**
The Zambezi Society,
Harare, Zimbabwe

Tchuma Tchato means "our wealth" in the chiKunda language and describes the vision that a community in Tete Province, Mozambique, holds about the value of the wild land and natural resources that fall within its influence.

The Tchuma Tchato project began in the 1990s, after the end of Mozambique's protracted civil war that left people's lives and livelihoods devastated by more than twenty years of unrest. It was conceived as a community-based natural resource management project

Fig. 8.1. Comboio Peak overlooks the Zambezi River Valley and Lake Cabora Bassa, Tete Province, Mozambique. Courtesy of The Zambezi Society

in an extremely remote and wild area south and west of Lake Cabora Bassa, the second-largest man-made impoundment on the Zambezi River in south-central Africa.

Originally established within the framework of the central government's agriculture, fisheries, forestry, and wildlife structures, with funding from the Ford Foundation, the project's aim was to work from the ground up to combine rural development with conservation. This involved empowering local people to value the land, wildlife, and other natural resources around them by realizing the potential and actual benefits gained from doing so, and to become responsible land stewards themselves. During the project's first ten years, the mechanisms for achieving this have been through sustainable resource use, notably fishing and sport hunting.

Since its inception, the Tchumo Tchato community concept has grown, and now extends its influence over much of the western part of Tete Province, including almost the entire Lake Cabora Bassa basin,

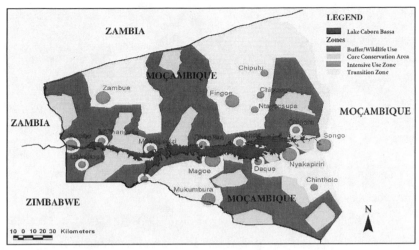

Fig. 8.2. The area of the proposed Tete Biosphere Reserve at the boundaries of Zimbabwe, Zambia, and Mozambique. Courtesy of The Zambezi Society

bordering the neighboring countries of Zambia, Zimbabwe, and Malawi. The involved communities have recently become major stakeholders in an ambitious biosphere reserve approach to development and management planning for the Tete area, with wilderness tourism as a key component.

The Tete Biosphere Approach

The Tete Biosphere Reserve, based on the UNESCO biosphere model, will cover approximately 4.8 million hectares (approximately 11.9 million acres) in the dry western half of Tete Province. It includes virtually the whole of Lake Cabora Bassa, stretching west of the town of Songo to its drainage basin north to the Zambian border, and south to the Zimbabwe border.

There is very little infrastructure in this entire region; there are few roads and formal settlements. The area has little rainfall, making it marginal for agriculture; consequently there are very few people in the area. Historically, people living here have depended on natural resources for survival. They have fished or hunted for thousands of years. Where agriculture has been practiced, it has been very much on a subsistence level. In global terms, this is Africa in its least developed state.

The long period of unrest and civil war following Mozambique's independence from Portugal exacerbated an already challenging situation for the people living in this part of Tete Province and curtailed development in the area for more than twenty years. When peace returned, communities had very few development options given the remoteness of their area, its extremely harsh climate, and its lack of infrastructure of any kind.

The Tchuma Tchato "our wealth" concept arose out of the sustainable resource use paradigm that was developed and popularized widely in southern African rural development circles during the 1990s. This philosophy recognizes that humans and human activity are an integral part of the ecosystem and have been so for several thousand years. It acknowledges that rural development is a priority and seeks to find ways to integrate people's needs with ensuring the long-term viability of the natural resources on which they depend.

Because few economically significant options were available for development in their area other than those based on natural resource assets, the Tete communities, in common with many other southern African community-focused development schemes, settled on sustainable resource use as their first-choice development option. Tchuma Tchato meant that communities would receive financial or material benefits from natural resource use to aid their development. This added value would encourage them to take on a stewardship role in protecting their natural resource assets from overexploitation. Commercial fishing for the introduced kapenta sardine was initiated on the lake to provide jobs and revenue for people living on its shores. Sport fishing opportunities began to attract a few intrepid tourism developers, who created fishing camps along the lakeshore, again providing jobs and revenue. Sport hunting for large animals, including elephants, attracted high-paying operators and their clients and brought associated infrastructure and benefits for local people.

The Need for Land Planning

However, as development pressures grew in the late 1990s, provincial authorities and local communities urgently needed to introduce land planning mechanisms if they were to take their stewardship and conservation obligations seriously. But they lacked the information required to make environmentally sensitive land planning decisions. With financial assistance from the Ford Foundation, which had played a major role in the formation of Tchuma Tchato, they engaged a regional nongovernmental organization—The Zambezi Society—to undertake an assessment of the biodiversity and wilderness values of Lake Cabora Bassa's shore and surrounding communal lands.

When the survey was completed in 2001, the Tete provincial authorities had a rough ecological and aesthetic guideline for land zoning. Funding from the European Union and the World Bank—together with initiatives by the Ford Foundation, the African Wildlife Foundation, and The Zambezi Society—have widened the planning and conservation focus in the past few years. Further ecological survey work has been undertaken north of the lake. Social, cultural, and historic perspectives have been considered, attempts have been made to address trans-boundary issues, and a growing awareness of the potential of the Cabora Bassa area as a low-density wilderness tourism destination has resulted.

The Biosphere Approach: Breaking New Ground

Today, there is broad agreement between the Tete government authorities, the Tchuma Tchato communities, major donors, and organizations working in the area that the best land use planning choice for the

Cabora Bassa basin will be to follow a biosphere approach using different zones for various land uses.

Although existing national legislation allows for state land designations that conform to standard applications such as reserves and national parks, this broader, more inclusive biosphere approach will break new ground in Mozambique.

Major Challenges: Land Rights and the Legal Status of Tchuma Tchato

While the biosphere approach is an exciting prospect for the development of western Tete Province and for the conservation of its wild lands, this approach faces many challenges, the most pressing of which are the issue of land tenure and the legal status of the Tchuma Tchato community initiative.

Although the government of Mozambique has recently recognized community rights to land and is allowing people to designate areas for their own management purposes, all land in the country is owned by the state. Securing land and resource tenure rights for the communities of western Tete Province is therefore a major initial focus of donor assistance for the establishment of the biosphere reserve. Areas will be delimited and registered under community title using newly introduced land law.

Furthermore, in order to strengthen its legal status, the Tchuma Tchato community is currently seeking to establish itself as an independent foundation in order to be better equipped to meet the challenges of the biosphere plan.

Land Management and Zoning

Another key step in establishing the Tete Biosphere Reserve—once the issues of land and resource tenure rights have been addressed—is for communities to identify land management options that they will regulate themselves. At present, no formal management plan for the proposed Tete biosphere area exists. However, the process of developing one is underway. Information about the land, its values, and resources has been gathered over the past decade and considerable consultation has occurred between communities, planners, developmental and conservation NGOs, government authorities, and donors.

Four main land uses have been identified and broad delineations mapped. They are:

- Intensive use zones where urban uses predominate, 160,000 hectares (395,000 acres);
- Transition zones where natural resource–based land use such as agriculture and mining takes place, 1.8 million hectares (4.5 million acres);
- Buffer zones where biodiversity harvesting (such as hunting, fishing, netting, kapenta harvesting, logging, and so forth) takes place on a managed and sustainable basis, 2 million hectares (4.9 million acres); and,
- Core areas that are of high conservation value and that act as refuges for biodiversity and have limited harvesting. These core areas supply surrounding areas with resources, and encompass 740,000 hectares (1.8 million acres). Core areas are similar to game reserves and supply a stream of resources such as fish or game animals to neighboring communities.

Developing the Potential for Wilderness Tourism

The people in western Tete Province are challenged by isolation, the ravages of civil war, a harsh climate, and wildness. But there is a growing awareness that these very challenges, together with their wealth of natural resources, are keys to improving living standards. The visible activities of community resource management projects like Tchuma Tchato and the support of many development and conservation well-wishers have helped to create a new spirit of developmental enterprise.

While living sustainably with wildlife has meant that hunting and fishing, either commercially or for sport, have long been the main income-generating activities for communities in the area, a new focus on marketing the Tete Biosphere's value as a wilderness tourism destination, particularly within those areas delineated as core and buffer zones, has been added.

African culture and wildlife coexist here in reality and are not simply museum pieces. It is a place where one comes face to face every day with the risks of wilderness: elephants, crocodiles, tsetse flies, thick mud, storms, and unpredictable winds. This very real wildness is complemented by the area's many natural features, a rich history and culture, and a virtually undeveloped man-made lake.

The idea is not to introduce mass tourism, but to attract adventure- and wilderness-seeking visitors to experience real Africa in its raw state—a place where modern man has tamed neither the climate, the wildlife, the insects, the land, nor the water. Within the biosphere concept, local communities will benefit and participate as partners in the development and management of the resources, earning wages for work and dividends for ownership in the developments.

Values to Attract Tourism

Survey data has identified the ecological, wilderness, cultural, and historical values that are so important to establishing a vision for tourism within the Tete Biosphere Reserve.

In 2002, The Zambezi Society played an important initial role in identifying areas with high biodiversity, high wilderness value, natural features of interest that might merit special conservation attention, and features that might be attractive to tourists. From this information, the land use zones were delineated and priority conservation areas (core and buffer zones) identified.

Natural Terrestrial Ecosystems

The Tete Biosphere Reserve area has a diverse mix of vegetation types providing a range of habitats for wild animal and bird species. Mixed woodland is most common, with the *mopane* species (*Coleospermum mopane*) dominating south of the lake and *miombo* woodland (mainly *Brachestegia* speciformis) dominating to the north.

When The Zambezi Society surveyed south of Lake Cabora Bassa, 301 plant species were identified, 58 of which were noted as being of potential conservation interest, including three near-endemic species: *Mimosa mossambicensis*, *Rhynchosia wildii*, and *Turraea zambesica*. The survey also broadly identified areas of biodiversity conservation interest and selected certain plant units as being most important for biodiversity conservation.

Birdlife and Wild Animals

The combination of the lake and the terrestrial ecosystems leads to a wide range of bird diversity in the area, with an interesting mix of central and southern African species. The Zambezi Society recorded 251 species south of Lake Cabora Bassa. Areas of particular interest for bird diversity and conservation priority were noted as those within a five-kilometer (three-mile) range of perennial water along the lakeshore, particularly on the alluvial flats and sandbanks, in the riparian forests along the area's major rivers, and in the cliff habitats of Cabora Bassa gorge.

Although the survey did not specifically record animal species, many of the wild animals associated with the Zambezi River

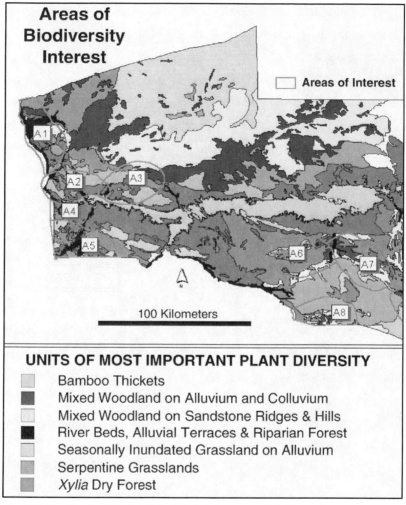

Fig. 8.3. The Zambezi Society identified eight areas of biodiverse interest,
labeled A1–A8, ranging from river beds, alluvial terraces, and riparian forests (A1)
to *Xylia* dry forests and serpentine grasslands (A8). Courtesy of The Zambezi
Society

Valley are present, including elephant, hippopotamus, buffalo, and
crocodile; predators including lion and hyena; various large and small
antelopes, as well as baboons, monkeys, and smaller mammal species.
Numbers are generally lower in comparison to other parts of the
Zambezi Valley.

Fig. 8.4. Elephants are a major attraction in the proposed biosphere reserve. They need careful management in order to avoid conflict with people. Courtesy of The Zambezi Society

Factors that may have contributed to the decline in wildlife numbers here include the long history of sport hunting in this area, more than two decades of civil war with little or no protection or management of wildlife, and issues of conflict between people and large animals such as elephants and lions. However, the activities of the Tchuma Tchato community-based natural resource management scheme, which provides benefits to people in exchange for their custodianship over wildlife, have recently led to a reduction in conflict and a relative increase in wildlife numbers.

Natural and Cultural Features of Interest

Although the Cabora Bassa impoundment is the result of a major hydroelectric dam across one of the Zambezi River's major gorges, the lake, with its extensive shoreline, provides a significant regional asset to the tourism industry. It is a large body of water, more than 350 kilometers (200 miles) long, with the Zambezi River flowing in at the extreme west. It provides a varied aquatic environment that supports abundant fish populations and attracts a diversity of aquatic birdlife and wild animals. While the lake is largely undeveloped, a comparison with Lake Kariba (upstream on the Zambezi), which has numerous resorts, camps, marinas, hotels, and is a major attraction for fishermen, shows the tourism development potential.

The area surrounding Lake Cabora Bassa has a diverse geomorphology and geology with some extremely interesting natural features that are either unique in their vegetation types, are centers of attraction for wildlife, or are inherently scenically attractive. As such, they add to the potential for tourism in the area. They include:

- the Luangwa River alluvial/colluvial fan northwest of the area;
- the Gonono Sand Ridge, which lies on the southern border with Zimbabwe;
- the Comboio Plateau—a vast, flat-topped hill feature dominating the Zambezi Valley southeast of the lake;
- the Luia River alluvium south of Comboio on the border with Zimbabwe; and,
- a number of hill features, including the prominent sandstone ridge running behind Magoe, Mount Bungue near Daque Camp, and Mount Ngosi on the north shore.

Wilderness Values

The combination of a diversity of ecological ecosystems, both terrestrial and aquatic, the scenic vistas associated with Lake Cabora Bassa and its shorelines, and the presence of wild animals and of interesting geological land features serves to create landscapes that are significant in terms of their wilderness values. The Zambezi Society survey also mapped broad areas of wilderness importance in the area.

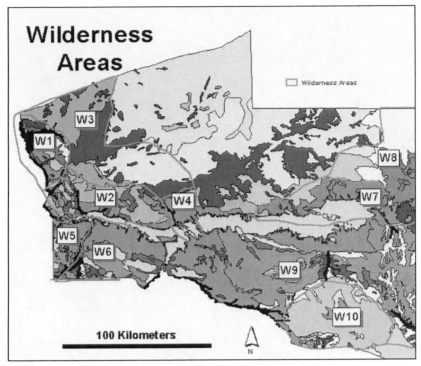

Fig. 8.5. The Zambezi Society identified ten areas of wilderness interest labeled W1–W10, such as the Comboio Plateau (W9) and the Luia alluvium (W10). Courtesy of The Zambezi Society

Cultural and Historical Values

In the interior of the Tete Biosphere area, away from the Zambezi River and the lake, the wild terrain, lack of roads, harsh climate, unproductive soils, and the presence of the tsetse fly, which prevents cattle-rearing, have meant that human settlement is very scattered and sparse. When there are villages, they tend to be small, the residents eking out an existence on subsistence agriculture or hunting—an isolated, traditional way of life that is disappearing in many urban African locations.

The greater part of the population is concentrated along the shores of Lake Cabora Bassa and along its major river tributaries.

However, even these settlements are not large. The predominant occupation here is fishing, and the main means of transport is water-based. Traditional cultural values and practices remain an important part of life in these remote communities. These could provide the basis for the development of some form of cultural tourism in the area.

Furthermore, the Zambezi River itself has a fascinating history as an important regional trade corridor and a focus for European imperialism and military activities, other major potential attractions of tourist interest. The Zambezi Valley played a key historical role in:

- The slave and ivory trade with Arabs and local tribes;
- The Portuguese trade route into the African interior, with a fort at Zumbo (at the extreme western end of what is now Lake Cabora Bassa), two at Tete, and others in Musandan and Muchena (believed to be the oldest European settlements in southern Africa);
- Zulu military history: a Zulu military expedition passed through the area;
- European missionaries' access to the interior: there is one German mission in Zumbo;
- The route of early European explorers, including David Livingstone, who visited a mission near Zumbo;
- Portuguese and other European colonialism; there are local Postos, villas, and churches;
- The Mozambiquan liberation war;
- The Zimbabwe liberation war ; and,
- The Mozambiquan civil war.

A Vision of Wilderness Tourism in the Tete Biosphere

Still very much at the conceptual stage, the vision for wilderness-based tourism within the biosphere area includes:

- Transportation: The dominant form of transport will be water-based, as it was in historical times. The area will also be accessible by four-wheel drive vehicles, boats, ferries, dhows, canoes, aircraft, and on foot. While there may be a lack of road transport, the Zambezi River and Lake Cabora Bassa provide a reliable and management-free water-based transport framework.
- Accommodations: Construction will be in period architecture, fitting in with the area's cultural history of African, Arab, and Portuguese colonial settlement, including Arab tented bush camps, African design luxury camps, Portuguese villas, and colonial houseboats.
- Tourism activities: Proposed tourism activities will be designed to fit into the existing land use, with game viewing, fishing, ethnobotanical adventures, game hunting, and sailing. The area offers a wide range of water- and land-based activities. The establishment of core conservation areas will attract resident wildlife and form the basis of a wildlife ecotourism industry that will include photographic safaris, bird-watching, wilderness trails, hiking, canoeing, sailing, and so forth. A network of buffer areas and conservation areas will provide a continuous network of linkages between tourist facilities that will offer opportunities for combining driving, sailing, boating, walking, and canoeing safaris.
- Cultural tourism: The presence of villages and people within the biosphere will make culture an integral part of the Tete Biosphere experience. The indigenous knowledge within the local communities can provide an additional service to tourists. Traditional understanding of vegetation or ethnobotany associated with rural villages offers a fascinating insight

into the culture and botany of the area. Guided tours of the local settlements and activities will provide an important additional income-earning opportunity. In addition, simple accommodations provided in these remote villages can also be a marketable service, especially for the drive-in tourists.

• Historical tourism: The rich local history provides another important service that can be traded. Various touring routes can be established to provide insight into the explorers who traveled through the area. The paths of the Nguni military campaigns, Portuguese explorers, and David Livingstone could be themes developed for tourists, incorporating a diversity of transport modes.

• Biodiversity conservation: Conservation areas will promote Tete biodiversity. The location of the core areas has been aligned with areas of high conservation value as identified by The Zambezi Society, and represents areas of international biodiversity significance. Mozambique could be a regional leader in biodiversity conservation by adopting the biosphere approach.

Fig. 8.6. A baobab forest grows on the slopes of Mount Bungwe to the south of Lake Cabora Basa. Courtesy of The Zambezi Society

- Water conservation (quality and quantity) and catchment management: The effective management of the Cabora Bassa basin will lead to increased water quantity, reduced sedimentation, and better water quality in the lake. This can result in significant cost savings for the hydroelectric scheme and other water users in the long run.

Benefits of the Tete Biosphere

- Local communities will benefit through a significant increase in income-earning opportunities, and through the provision of resources for further development, both natural and social. The increased demand for additional goods and services, such as fresh vegetables, building, and guiding, will further enhance the benefits of a biosphere.
- The national government will benefit by establishing a clear land use plan, which will facilitate rapid and consistent decision making with regard to development activity in the basin. The management system that is likely to emerge will closely involve district and provincial government personnel and will facilitate regular communication.
- Investors will benefit by having greater security for their investments as the quality of the natural assets will be maintained. In addition, the establishment of the Tete Biosphere with clear development zones and guidelines will limit the potential for conflicting land uses. For example, ecotourism, hunting, and commercial fishing will be separated, reducing conflicts of interest.
- Farmers, foresters, and fishermen will benefit by having access to greater resources for use or for development. Good management systems are able to keep natural

resource stocks at relatively high levels, providing opportunities for optimal harvesting levels.

- The scientific community will benefit from the establishment of a major site of cultural and biodiversity conservation, which will provide opportunities for research. Scientists and their backers are likely to want to support the Tete Biosphere with research experience and funds. There will be a real opportunity to develop a University of Eduardo Mondlane field station, which would support, coordinate, and participate in research in the area.

- The world community will benefit from the establishment of the Tete Biosphere and the significant cultural and biodiversity heritage that it will maintain. Furthermore, the size of the biosphere will promote the conservation of major natural landscapes and ecological systems that are not possible in small areas. Establishing a working model for sustainable development will be of major interest to the international community and is likely to attract significant support.

- The biosphere approach may also be a strategic model for other regions in the country where natural resource use is a

Fig. 8.7. The Comboio Plateau rises at the southern edge of the proposed biosphere reserve. Courtesy of The Zambezi Society

foundation of local economic development, and where the sustainability of the resources and culture are in the interests of both local and national government.

The Tete Biosphere Implementation Strategy

A strategy has been developed for the establishment of a biosphere. A three-phase approach is proposed that first determines the extent of local and provincial interest in the concept. Once—and if there is a positive response from the local and provincial governments—it will then be necessary to develop a business plan to implement the biosphere. The resulting business plan would form the basis of fund-raising to implement the third phase, the establishment of the reserve. The steps in each of the three phases are outlined below.

Phase One: Identifying participating communities, districts, and areas

1. Identify key players

- Administrators and communities in Magoe, Zumbo, Cahora Bassa, and Maravia
- Tete Provincial Government
- Tchuma Tchato
- Mozambique National Government
- World network of biospheres, UNESCO
- Interested and affected parties

2. Engage stakeholders and interested and affected parties

- Identify participating communities and their areas
- Amend general concepts
- Identify broad biosphere boundaries

3. Develop a funding proposal for Phase Two
- Undertake a task analysis of the jobs in Phase Two
- Budget the tasks identified

Phase Two: Implementation and business plan for the Tete Biosphere

Once funds have been secured:

1. Create development and management policies based on the resource, tourism markets, and legal assessments, generate principles for development in consultation with stakeholders. The following aspects should be addressed:
- Determine policies in consultation with stakeholders
- Define natural resources use and management policy
- Define tourism development policy

2. Identify and map biolsphere boundaries and zones
- Identify development, multiple use, and conservation zones.
- Create a detailed zoning plan.
- Boundary survey and demarcation

3. Create tourism and natural resources use and management plans. Examples of a number of key aspects are:
- Institutional arrangements
- Ownership arrangements for areas and facilities
- Management committees for coordinating implementation
- Benefit-sharing mechanisms between enterprises and communities
- Staffing of management and coordinating agencies
- Operational financing arrangements
- Reserve demarcation and core and buffer areas management plans

- Wildlife management centers, such as field stations and outposts
- Fire management policies and strategies
- Game and vegetation monitoring
- Fish population monitoring
- Hunting and fishing licensing and control
- Tourism development planning
- Tourism themes—historical, cultural, and ecological experiences
- Tourism use zone—development nodes and activity areas
- Accommodation themes and locations
- Investor marketing program
- Environmental management—waste management, resource use, and so forth in all zones
- Transport infrastructure
- Water routes
- Ferries
- Harbors
- Roads
- Airstrips

Phase Three: Develop business/financing plan for management and development institutions

Challenges and Limitations

Many challenges face the communities, authorities, donors, and implementors in creating the Tete Biosphere Reserve. These can be roughly divided into those posed by the physical environment itself and those posed by factors affecting the investment environment.

- The biophysical environment is harsh, especially in the wet season, and will limit tourist development options in the region. This area is unlikely to attract mass tourism. Only the most adventurous wilderness-seeking visitors are likely to come. Challenging factors include:

1. The relative lack of wild animals, especially in the eastern gorge section of Cabora Bassa;
2. Environmental degradation, especially adjacent to the Cabora Bassa gorge;
3. Overexploitation of fish resources through netting;
4. Existence of remnant land mines from the war years in certain areas;
5. Land-based travel is not possible during the wet season of December through February;
6. Malaria is a very real limitation; and,
7. Regional competition for tourism in Zambia, Malawi, Zimbabwe, and other parts of Mozambique.

However, the climate, remoteness, and limited road access should be used as an opportunity for developing a unique tourism product. The area should have a wilderness adventure focus rather than being marketed as mass tourism for families. A land use plan should be developed and implemented to prevent environmental degradation, unplanned tourism operations, and conflicts. Resource management plans should be developed for game, fish, and vegetation use, using the Tchuma Tchato model. Clear information on risks and regulations should be provided to potential visitors.

- The investment environment in the region is currently very risky. It discourages large-scale investors and is only suitable for small, high-risk investors. The situation also encourages a short-term approach to investment, in which investors need to get their returns as fast as possible because their circumstances may change at short notice. This does not promote a focus on developing long-term relationships with neighboring communities. Particularly challenging factors include:

1. excessive bureaucracy, delays, and frustrations;
2. lack of information and few guidelines on investment opportunities, legal requirements, or duty-free incentives;
3. absence of an investor-friendly attitude and environment;
4. lack of land tenure and long-term investment options;
5. shortage of skilled labor, construction materials, and basic food essentials mean expensive imports;
6. inefficiency and lack of tourism promotion by government, immigration, or law enforcement authorities;
7. environmental impacts are often being considered too late in the developmental process;
8. lack of clear licensing policies for tourist boating, fishing, and so forth; and,
9. little English is spoken by officials who deal with investors and visitors.

The investment environment needs to be made more secure and investor-friendly. An investment framework with strict time schedules needs to be developed. Local business and industry needs to be promoted along with training initiatives for local people. The provincial director of tourism and the provincial governor should coordinate the activities of other key departments that can promote tourism.

The establishment of a biosphere to effectively guide development and land use activities is strongly recommended. Such an organized system with clear guidelines would also promote investor confidence and attract serious investors with long-term perspective, who would encourage the development of the tourism industry as a whole.

Chapter 9

~~~~~~~~~~~~~~~~

The Toda Relationship
with Wild Nature:
Indicators of Ecosystem Health
in Tamil Nadu State, India

Tarun Chhabra,
Founder, Edhkwehlynawd Botanical Refuge,

Nilgiris, India

Editor's Note: Much of this case study also appears as "How Traditional Ecological Knowledge Addresses Global Climate Change: The Perspective of the Todas—the Indigenous People of the Nilgiri Hills of South India" by Tarun Chhabra, found as a pdf file at the Society for Ecological Restoration International and Indigenous Peoples' Restoration Network: www.ser.org/iprn/eitproject.asp (accessed 2/20/2008).

For the Toda people, their relationship with nature begins at birth when the newborn is a silent participant at elaborate birth ceremony rites. A number of plant species are used during the ceremony, highlighted by holding an "umbrella" of *Mahonia leschenaultiana* over the mother and newborn to protect them from the destructive influence of the star Keihhtt. In fact, the baby's face is not exposed to the outdoors until the naming ceremony, several months after birth. At the naming rites, the child's face is ceremonially exposed by his

Fig. 9.1. A Toda mother and newborn, whose face is covered. The Toda people's relationship with nature begins at birth with a ceremony using plants to protect the mother and child from the destructive influence of the star Keihhtt. Courtesy of Tarun Chhabra

grandfather in front of the hamlet's dairy temple.

After prostrating at the temple, the parents present the baby and tell him/her the sacred names of all the major natural sites around the hamlet. These are purely representative and include one example of a sacred peak, stream, buffalo, bird, animal, temple, tree, and other sites or animals the baby will relate reverentially to during its lifetime. Thus begins every Toda's relationship with sacred nature.

The Toda historical and mythological connection with nature began soon after their dreamtime. During this time, the gods lived among the Todas. Each of the gods' life stories is well known, and natural landmarks associated with their exploits still exist. After their time, these gods and goddesses went on to occupy various hill summits, where they are still believed to reside. There are more than thirty *taihhow tehtt*, or deity peaks. Even today, an elder would not commit the sacrilege of pointing out the location of a deity peak with his finger; he instead points at a neighboring hill and says, "The peak next to that." Therefore, the earliest Toda sacred connection with nature began when their gods took up residence in certain prominent peaks.

A typical Toda prayer consists of sacred chant words, or *kwa(r)shm*, to different natural landmarks, which might include nearby peaks, slopes, valleys, ridges, shola thickets, sacred trees, sacred rocks, swamps, meadows, pools, streams, the area beside the dairy temple, sacred buffalo pens, pen-posts, and pen-post bars. There is a body of several hundred sacred natural features in all prayers. Of the natural landmarks, the peaks are the most sacred entities, each representing either a major or a local deity.

In addition to the deity peaks, there are hills that are sacred to all Todas but exceptionally sacred to individual clans, to which they are almost on par with the deity peaks. The Taihkavfy hill for the Taihhfakh clan and the Tehhkolmudry hill (where the gods used to hold council in ancient times) for the Kerrir clan are prominent examples of such locally sacred hills. Then there are the numerous hills that are sacred to a single hamlet and temple. Finally, there are hills situated in the Toda afterworld of Amunawdr. Here, the hill of the ruling deity Aihhn is called Taihh mushkullnn.

Todas believe that sacred peaks are anthropomorphic representations of particular deities, and hence they do not build shrines on summits, although other groups have occasionally constructed shrines in later times. Todas passing in the vicinity of a deity peak reverentially perform the *koymukht* salutation and softly chant the sacred prayer words of that god. Kwatteihhn and Kawnttaih are the only two peaks visited on a pilgrimage by a few Todas. Many Todas relate stories of hearing a god entering a hill and closing the entrance. At Kawllvoy, close to Pazhtaarr hamlet, the door-like entrance into the hill can be seen.

Several stories relate the power of specific gods, both from ancient and more recent times. One recent story describes the construction of a hydroelectric dam at upper Bhavani a few decades ago. Workers started digging earth from the nearby deity hills of Aihhzaihow and Mozaihow. Several Toda elders protested the sacrilege, but their words were not heeded. After some time came the news that during the digging work, the earth had caved in and killed some workers. These hills were not touched thereafter.

Any alteration, such as planting exotic trees, tea, or physical destruction as mentioned above, in the ecosystem around a deity hill is an indication of profound sickness of the environment. It is imperative to persuade the government to declare all deity hills and their surroundings as indigenous heritage sites so that they are inviolable in the future.

The second major Toda connection with nature began when the goddess Taihhki(r)shy divided her people into patrilineal clans, of which fifteen still exist. After creating the clans, Taihhki(r)shy brought forth the buffaloes by a miraculous process. She divided them into secular domestic herds and sacred temple herds. She then created a number of grades of sacred temples and ordained which clans were to own which grade of temple. She stated which people were allowed to serve as priests for the various grades of temples, and she created a particular grade of sacred buffalo herd for each of the temple categories. She also gave the *kwa(r)shm*, or sacred words, to all the sacred areas and sites. In summary, she laid down the rules that form the rituals of today. She also established a sacred relationship with numerous aspects of surrounding nature, and gave prayer names.

Taihhki(r)shy's father is the god Aihhn, who rules the afterworld from the peak called Taihh mushkullnn. Aihhn told Taihhki(r)shy that he had decided to create an afterworld (Amunawdr) where Todas would live on after death. He asked his daughter to look after the existing world (Imunawdr).

All men, buffaloes, and trees then came to bid farewell to Aihhn. On his way to the afterworld, Aihhn took a strange path. He climbed up a series of natural rocky steps, cooked food at a site, and rested. He touched his chest on a stone and forgot all worldly attachments. Finally, after a long trek across many natural obstacles, he reached the area where he set up the realm of the departed.

Aihhn then established that after scrupulously observing essential rituals from birth to the funeral ceremonies, a Toda's spirit is eligible to depart to Amunawdr, following the same route across the same natural landmarks that Aihhn crossed. The ceremonies specific to men are the priest's ordination rituals; for women, they are the rituals of pregnancy. Thus, if a young girl dies, pregnancy rituals are incorporated in the funeral ceremony so that the spirit goes to Amunawdr to dwell peacefully.

This set of rituals defines the third major Toda relationship with nature. It establishes that only a Toda who has performed all his or her lifetime sacred rites, using all the mandatory plants, is qualified to reside in the afterworld. As long as the Todas continue to believe in the afterworld and the journey there, their culture is likely to survive.

The fifteen or so landmarks that the spirit is supposed to cross en route to the afterworld exist as landmarks in the physical world. For example, the stone steps that the spirit ascends are a stupendous flight of natural steps going through the center of an awe-inspiring vertical cliff face.

Natural Sacred Sites
Waters
Rivers

There are two major river systems in the western Nilgiris; both are highly sacred to the Todas. The first is now called the Mukurti-Pykara system, or Kawlykeen by the Todas. This mighty river has its source in the Mukurti region, a high-rainfall area known to receive up to 10,000 millimeters (394 inches or nearly 33 feet) of rainfall per year, mostly over just two months.

The Todas have an interesting story of origin for this river. In ancient times, the priest at the highest grade of temple dairy committed a transgression of sacred rules. He harvested some honey from a tree cavity and planned to hoard it without sharing. As he was walking down the slope, the handle fastened to the bamboo honey vessel snapped, and honey began to flow from the broken vessel. As the honey flowed, it turned to water and marked the source of a river. The stream that this story is attributed to can still be seen as the river's source.

The bamboo vessel, on breaking, became a snake. The snake looked menacingly at the priest, who became terrified and started to run. The snake gave chase to the errant priest for a short distance. As he ran, the priest noticed a hare crossing his path. He instinctively threw his sacred black loincloth onto the hare. The snake, thinking the hare to be the priest, continued chasing the cloth-covered hare for a long distance, but was unable to catch hold of the fast hare. The priest was saved.

Fig. 9.2. The Todas regard many rivers in the Nilgiri Hills as sacred and believe they must be kept wild and free. Courtesy of Tarun Chhabra

The stream that flowed from the spilled honey became the original source of the Mukurti-Pykara rivers, and the shola thicket at the slopes of the Tehhdhykeihn hill lies at the source of this sacred river. The route that was first taken by the snake and the priest, followed by the snake and the covered hare, went on to form the course of this river. Hence at the origin, this river is called Koylkwehhdr paw, from which the general name of the entire river, Kawlykeen, is derived. *Koyl* means bamboo, and refers to the bamboo vessel that fell and from which the sacred honey started to leak. The hare was chased up to a point near the Glenmorgan area, believed to be the area where the river loses its sanctity and flows down the slopes. The hare escaped at this point and the river is called Kadrtashpaw at the end. In prayers, this river is referred to as Kawlykeen/Kavozerry.

In the past, this river was held to be exceptionally sacred. Todas crossing it must not be in a state of impurity, and have to follow certain rules and guidelines to cross. They could cross only on certain days of the week, and while doing so, must have their right shoulders uncovered (*kefehnaarr*). There are certain specified crossing points, different for laypeople and for priests.

There is a well-known song composed within the past few hundred years at the funeral of a man named Marvoy, who, after engaging in coitus, crossed this river and went to collect honey at Mudhmarr hill, violating both the sanctity of the river and the sacred act of honey gathering. Only when vultures were seen hovering some days later did his relatives set out to search for him. A tiger had killed him, and the song composed at his funeral describes his life and death in detail. Todas can still point out the steep rock where Marvoy searched for the hive before the tiger meted out justice.

The other major river system of the western Nilgiris also has legendary roots in honey gathering. This is the Avalanche-Emerald reservoir of today, or Kinatthill(zh)y in Toda.

Rules and stories like these maintain the sanctity of these rivers. Unfortunately, sacred crossing points no longer hold much relevance in the daily lives of Todas, because the waters of the Pykara hydroelectric reservoir have submerged them. Younger Todas do not even know the names and locations of the crossing points. Outsiders have no idea that the extreme sanctity of this river is all but lost due to damming. In addition to the Pykara and Mukurti dams, associated dams and reservoirs at Porthimund and Glenmorgan have obliterated many hamlets and sacred temples, sacred migratory paths, seasonal hamlets, and most of the sacred Tee temples. Even today, when a Toda diviner is asked a question relating to the many problems that beset Todas nowadays, the answer is often linked to the abandonment of the Tee complexes.

As mentioned, the Toda gods and goddesses are believed to reside in certain sacred hills. The only exception is the abode of Awlvoy at a sacred waterfall in the Pykara river, indicating the veneration with which that river is treated. The damming of two sacred river systems may have led to a surge in hydroelectric power generation for India's Tamil Nadu State, but it also, by a series of cruel blows, severed the most important link that the Todas had with these deity rivers. Since these rivers no longer run wild, there is no real sanctity remaining. The sacred crossing points do no exist anymore, except when they flow out from a dam or during the dry season when water has been released from the reservoir. During this time, devout Todas still recognize and pray at the crossing points. As far as the rivers of the upper Nilgiris are concerned, the Todas believe that their ecosystem has suffered irreparable damage.

Sacred Streams, Pools, and Springs

Every Toda hamlet with a dairy temple has sacred streams. One is the ordination stream, used in priesthood rituals. Another is the sacred dairy temple stream, where the priest draws water for his daily use and for cooking. This is called *pol(zh)y neepaw*, although each has a separate *kwa(r)shm* used by the priest in the prayer of the specific temple. If a hamlet has two or three temples, there is usually a stream for each, although sometimes a single stream may be used for more than one purpose. In this case, the higher course of the same stream is used for the more sacred temple. No person other than a priest or a priest-to-be can touch the waters of these two categories of streams. When a temple is reoccupied or if the water is deemed to have been polluted, the stream is purified by the priest with *tehhdr* bark. Most sacred hamlets also have another stream for sacred salt-pouring rites held during the year. Again, only a priest is allowed to draw water to dissolve the salt.

In some temples of exceptional sanctity, like the Konawsh conical temple, a separate stream is reserved for Toda men to bathe and purify themselves before approaching the temple. These streams should be perennial, as most temples operate during the dry season. The ecosystem is said to be in ill health, generally attributed to an alteration in the ecosystem, if sacred streams run dry. Possible reasons could be pollution by extraneous elements; the transgression of sacred rules by the priest; or, in modern times, changes in climatic patterns, especially those related to the southwest monsoon.

At migratory hamlets like Teihhfakh, a stream is reserved for guests to use for festive cooking on the migration day. Every hamlet also has a nonsacred stream for regular domestic use. The segregation of sacred and domestic streams is marked, and often a priest who returns to his hamlet touches the domestic stream as a final act of becoming a layman.

In addition to the sacred and the domestic, there are other categories of streams. One is connected with the dreamtime, when the Toda gods dwelled in the Nilgiris. For example, the pool Nehrykaihhrr, where the goddess Taihhki(r)shy created the buffaloes, is mentioned in the prayer of the conical temple at nearby Pawshaihh (Nawsh). Similarly, the stream called Naihhrrotkwehhdr, where the god Kwattaihh tied down the reflection of the sun and made daylight into darkness, is mentioned in the prayer of the conical temple at Konawsh. Also, we have sacred streams or pools associated with the gods that are not mentioned in prayers. For example, the pool in the stream Polpaw, near the Kurumba hamlet of Pawny (Tudiki), is said to be where the god Kwatteihhn came across the goddess Teihhkosh bathing. We once came across this amazing pool—shaped like a circular buffalo pen and engulfed in divine vibrations—after a long and arduous trek.

We have a singular example of a waterfall called Awllvoy that is classified as a deity site; almost all the other landmarks on this list are deity peaks. This waterfall is mentioned in many prayers. Finally, we have a number of streams and pools that are connected with the after-world Amunawdr. One example is the stream Waskonskwehhdr, where the departing female spirit places her pestle into a mortar-shaped pit within the stream. Another is the large stream Pufehrrkheen, where the spirit crosses a thread bridge en route to the afterworld.

Only when one has experienced the energy levels of these sacred waters can one understand the sanctity that Todas have tradi-tionally attached to them. The pool where Kwatteihhn came upon the goddess bathing is a fine example. Another example occurred at the now-abandoned hamlet of Kashwehh, belonging to the Kerrir clan; its sacred dairy spring is called Ooneer. Since ancient times, only the priest has drawn water from this pool. Now that the hamlet is not occu-pied, other people may occasionally use this water, advised to do so with utmost reverence. For eight years, I have visited this abandoned hamlet to observe periods of solitude in the wilderness. This sacred spring nearly always has water, even during the driest months. Only twice was it observed to have run dry—both times during the wet season. Once, this was traced to a non-Toda buffalo herder whose daughter had drawn water during menstruation. Soon after the rituals were performed to sanctify this pool, the water returned.

Sacred waters are important indicators of the well-being of the Toda homeland; in many cases, the temples cannot be operated otherwise.

Wetlands

The Todas have scores of swamps that are highly venerated and have sacred prayer names. These have also undergone profound changes in recent times, invariably for the worse. With the damming of sacred rivers, many of the largest wetlands were inundated and vast areas of extremely rich biological diversity were destroyed. These swamps have also been destroyed or altered by agriculture, planting of exotic trees, overgrazing, lack of burning—either naturally or in Toda rituals—and climatic changes affecting the southwest monsoon. The main indication that Toda wetlands have been taken over by invasive plants is the progressive and alarming decline of the endemic grass used to thatch Toda temples.

Sholas

Sholas are thickets in the upper Nilgiris composed of stunted montane evergreen trees that hold a variety of epiphytic flora including orchids, a forest floor containing a number of rare and endangered flora like wild balsams, and a stream. The Toda relationship with sholas can be sacred; many contain specific divine objects like trees, rocks, pools, streams, and sacred pathways used only by priests. The connection is also utilitarian; sholas house many important flora used in various ceremonies and aspects of traditional life.

Grasslands

The grassy downs that surround sholas contain sacred pastures, slopes, rocks, streams, milking grounds, and other important sites mentioned in prayers. They also contain floral species vital to various aspects of Toda life. Indeed, the sholas and grasslands of the upper Nilgiris actually constitute the basis of the Toda ecosystem. Without them, there would be no water and no biodiversity. As we shall see in the section on flora, the absence of water and of important floral species normally housed in these climax ecosystems indicates a degradation of their vitality. This degradation can be attributed to actual destruction, planting of exotic trees, agriculture, climate change, or habitation.

Rocks

In and around every sacred hamlet and site, one finds interesting rocks and stones. Many of these are sacred and have names that are chanted in prayers. Some also have utilitarian aspects, like the specific rocks on which salt is ground for ceremonies. Others are associated with specific rituals performed by priests, such as pouring freshly drawn milk from sacred buffaloes. Some were placed in ancient times to form the walls of either sacred buffalo pens or temples.

Many have interesting mythological stories describing miraculous origins. For example, a couple is said to have gone on a pilgrimage while in a state of impurity, and were thus turned to stone. Two vertical rocks show them looking in different directions, just like the story narrates. The site where a god is supposed to have made a steep stream flow backward by damming it, to show the other gods that he was their equal, still has a huge cylindrical rock by the side of the stream.

By treating various categories of rocks as sacred, the Todas are able to protect various aspects of their ecosystem. Added to this is the fact that many of these sacred rocky areas are essentially repositories of perennial mountain springs and streams. In protecting such zones by declaring them as sacred, the Todas have been able to offset, to a large extent, the effects of climatic changes that might otherwise have led to the drying up of water sources. Declaring the waters as sacred is not always sufficient, so the Todas have also declared many rocks and cliffs as divine.

In addition to the natural sites mentioned, some areas combine natural and man-made features, such as sacred hamlets that house temple complexes of the highest grades. In these places, like the area around the Konawsh conical temple complex, everything is sacred. In addition to the temple, the surrounding shola, grassland, waters, flora, specific rocks, pathways, buffalo pens, hills, and other landmarks are all considered sacred. One has to approach this area barefoot and in a state of purity. Relieving oneself is prohibited.

We therefore see that the Todas treat various sites with differing gradations of sanctity. Sacred Toda areas maintain a healthy ecosystem and resultant microclimate, insulating them from the effects of global climate change. Only in modern times, when the government has disallowed Todas from managing the ecosystem as they have done proficiently for millennia, has the fabric of ecological health begun to disintegrate. The Nilgiri ecosystem has withdrawn from its climax status. However, it still houses phenomenal biological diversity. The government should take steps to restore it to its hallowed standing.

Sacred Animals and Plants

Fauna

Various faunal species have also been conserved and protected by the Todas in a twofold method. The first is the animals' status as sacred—albeit, in some cases, feared—creatures. Also, the Toda practice of vegetarianism, which is most unusual in a community that did not practice agriculture and where even today game is abundant, protected the fauna. Todas have a name and story for almost every animal and bird in their area.

Todas herd and breed buffalo that are endemic to the Nilgiris. As previously discussed, these are separated into sacred and domestic herds. Each of the six grades of temple dairies has an associated grade of buffalo that can only be milked by the priest of that particular temple grade. The priest incorporates a complex series of rituals into the seemingly mundane procedure of churning milk into various milk products. Buffaloes are the most sacred and important facet of life to Todas.

Animals play other important roles in Toda tradition. The son of the god Kwatteihhn was carried away by a tiger for failing to adhere to temple regulations. We have seen how a tiger killed a man in more recent times for crossing a sacred river in a state of impurity. Even today, we are told of many instances of tigers meting out justice when an errant priest thought that no one had noticed his transgressions.

Fig. 9.3. A Nilgir tahr, an endangered species. Courtesy of Tarun Chhabra

Birds have a similar, although more varied, role. The bird that warns people of transgression of sacred rules is the pied bushchat (*Saxicola caprata*), *kaarrpill(zh)c* in Toda. Because the female of this species looks different, it has a separate name. This bird warned the god Aihhn's son of a sacred regulation that he had omitted. This warning was not heeded, and the son met his end by drowning. The mighty god Kwatteihhn himself was warned by this bird that he was getting too close to a goddess bathing in a pool.

The gray jungle fowl (*Gallus sonneratii*) was the companion of some gods and plays a traditional role of rousing them—and us—from sleep. The gods bestowed beauty upon them in return. The Egyptian vulture (*Neophron percnopterus*) is a divine messenger, often from the after-world. This bird sat atop the head of an old lady belonging to the Kerrir clan when they were on the brink of extinction, helping her conceive. The house sparrow (*Passer domesticus*) helps to control the severity and duration of the monsoon. The common kestrel (*Falco tinnunculus*) and the Oriental honey-buzzard (*Pernis ptilorhyncus*) lead Todas toward new sources of honey.

Certain birds like the streak-throated woodpecker (*Picus xanthopygaeus*) and one species of owl are harbingers of ill fortune and are avoided. Others like the white-cheeked barbet (*Megalaima viridis*) call to indicate the time of day. The greater coucal (*Centropus sinensis*) has the uncanny ability to locate rare herbs from remote mountaintops inaccessible to man; the Todas use these birds to lead them to medicinal plants.

Fig. 9.4. A pied bushchat (*Saxicola caprata*), a bird believed by the Todas to warn people of transgressing sacred rules. Todas protect and conserve animal species by considering them sacred and by practicing vegetarianism. Courtesy of Tarun Chhabra

We have seen how an errant priest was chased by a snake in ancient times, leading to the formation of one of the most sacred rivers. Todas believe that certain snakes take care of sacred temples, especially in the absence of a priest. These snakes also warn priests when sacred transgressions are being committed.

With insects, the Todas have long understood the specific pollinators of flowering species, as this helped them collect honey.

Flora

The intimate connection with flora illustrates the dependence of the Toda people on their ecosystem. Maintenance of ecosystem health includes:

1. Marking all natural resources, notably the flora, which have a traditional religious use. Each of these species has a sacred prayer name and must be used in a sustainable manner. The Todas do so by remaining within the natural cycle and keeping their own human population levels low, even today restricted to the self-imposed population limit of 1,400.

2. Using specific floral species in various ritual ceremonies. Since these cannot be substituted, these species must be abundant around all hamlets. The most important uses that Todas have for the plants in their homeland are cultural. Every ritual or ceremony is centered on the use of specific species of plants. One reason the Todas have preserved their ecosystem is their dependence upon these plants for cultural practices.

   Why have these people preserved their cultural ethos? Because of the belief that only a person who has performed the mandatory lifetime rituals is qualified to take residence at the afterworld Amunawdr. As long as this belief persists, the Todas will preserve their culture and will strive to preserve their environment. For example, pregnancy and paternity rites entail the use of the following plants: *Arundinaria* species of bamboo reeds; *Mappia foetida* leaves; *Rhododendron arboreum* subspecies Nilagiricum sticks; *Rubus ellipticus* leaves; *Myrsine capitellata* branches; *Syzygium arnottianum*; *Sophora glauca* branches; and *Andropogon schoenanthus* grass. If all the species used in a Toda's rituals and culture were to be counted, more than one hundred plant species are required in the vicinity of each hamlet.

3. Using specific plants in the construction of traditional structures. Toda barrel-vaulted and conical temples are constructed using specific forest species like *kwehtf* or *paarsh* (*Sideroxylon* species) tree poles; specified wooden planks or stone slabs; rattan cane (*Calamus pseudo-tenuis*); *waadr* bamboo reeds (*Arundinaria wightiana* and *A. w.* var. hispida); specified wood for the door and carved *kweghaishveil* (a ritual item like a totem that is placed vertically on top of the thatch); *teff*, thin bamboo reeds (*Pseudoxytenanthera monadelpha*); and a swamp grass called *avful*. If any of these once-plentiful species were depleted, the Toda culture would be at a crossroads, because they may not substitute another species. Taken a step further, if any of these were to become locally extinct, Toda culture could collapse in a short period. This is a frightening scenario, given that Toda culture is unique, as are their barrel-vaulted and conical temples and houses.

Only two conical temples remain, one of which was rebuilt in 1995. It took some time to convince the clansmen of the need to rebuild this structure and keep the unique rituals alive. Now, the conical temple of Konawsh is opened every year for a month for ritual purposes. Such temples are veritable marvels of tribal architecture. Even in areas where annual precipitation can exceed 3,000 millimeters (118 inches), they can last for up to eighty years, requiring only periodic rethatching.

The grass used to thatch Toda temples illustrates the predicament that these people find themselves in today. Excluding a few hamlets in the east, Todas are only allowed to use a species of grass called *avful* for building. As recently as a quarter of a century ago, this grass was fairly common in many swamps in the main Toda heartland of Wenlock Downs. Today, it has nearly disappeared from this area, and can be found in reasonable quantity only in some large swamps in the extreme western plateau, specifically Korakundah and surrounding areas. Even here, another species dominates.

What are the reasons for the disappearance of this species from most of the swampy areas? A recent study showed that ever since the Todas were prohibited from setting fire to these swamps, a way of Toda management by a sacred ritual, other species soon took over. The mass planting of exotic trees like eucalyptus and wattle on adjacent hillsides have also contributed.

The avful species was finally identified as *Eriochrysis rangacharii*, C.E.C. Fischer, a Nilgiri endemic mentioned in the red data book of endangered species. In fact, even though the Todas have used this regularly to thatch their temples, it was thought by science to be almost extinct some decades ago. It is also the only Indian representative of an otherwise African and American genus. The project to formally identify this species was sponsored by The WILD Foundation.

4. Using specific indicator species to show different facets of the Toda way of life and their link with nature.

  • Certain species indicate the seasons in a year, and each stage within every season. For example, the indicator species for the immediate premonsoon phase are *avfulazhky* and *nicazhky*—both belonging to the *Oldenlandia* genus and ubiquitous in May. An ancient song and story refer to a sacred buffalo that came to this world from Amunawdr and calved when the flowers of these two bushes were blooming. From this, we know that the story took place during the month of May. The name *avfulazhky* literally means puffed rice, derived from the appearance of the unopened buds of this plant. Other plants that flower during this period are the different species of *Arisaema* or "cobra flowers," called *poddwa(r)shk*. The early monsoon is indicated by *Ceropegia pusilla* (the "churning stick" plant), *Drosera peltata* (an insectivorous sundew), and the orchid *Calanthe triplicata* (the leaves are used to hold honey). The delicate *Anemone rivularis* flowers during the peak monsoon. The final phase is represented by the most handsome of all Nilgiri wildflowers, the Nilgiri lily (*Lilium neilgherrense*).

    The last phase of the monsoon, in early September, is also the most punishing. I once told a Toda elder, Kwattawdr Kwehhttn, that the rains showed no signs of abating, and he assured me that the monsoon would end within a week. He explained that the sacred *maw(r)sh* trees (*Michelia nilagirica*) had started flowering en masse in the sholas, indicating the impending end of the southwest monsoon. Other seasons and intervening stages are similarly indicated by specific species by their flowering cycles.

To a Toda, their ecosystem is in good stead if all indicator species flower at the precise time that the corresponding stage of each season commences or ends. Recently, alteration in the hilltop ecology where the Nilgiri lily and churning stick plants are located has caused them to become scarce. Similar examples indicate a change in the health of the environment.

• Other species indicate the climatic pattern of a particular period of the year. The Todas have terms for the differing climatic variations that every season brings, marked by the flowering of corresponding plant species. The relationship does not end here: the climatic pattern of that period, the species flowering, and the star most prominent in the sky during the period all have identical names. The ecosystem is therefore said to be healthy only if all elements of this climate-flower-star triad are in perfect synchronicity. Any change in climatic pattern first affects the flowering cycle of the indicator species. For example, a change in the intensity of the southwest monsoon in recent years has caused the peak monsoon indicator (*Anemone* species) not to bloom in profusion, but very sporadically.

• Certain species are associated with prominent stars visible in the evening and night sky during a particular period, as explained above. By early October, the premonsoon showers from the northeast monsoon commence, causing a peculiar weather pattern. Fragmented showers of rain give way to clear sky; this is called *kaashtk*. A star of this name is visible in the night sky and an exquisite flower (*Exacum bicolour*) called *kaashtk* simultaneously flowers abundantly. The Todas have twenty-eight star-weather-plant triads representing different phases of the year. Plants in the genus *Impatiens* or *nawtty* are part of this series. Changes in these triads not only show that the indicator species and the climate have been disturbed, but changes in cloud cover mean that the corresponding star may not be as visible either.

- Certain species like *Strobilanthes* and some bamboos flower in precise cycles. As long as they continue to do so at precise intervals (the Todas are aware of the number of years after which each of these should bloom), the ecosystem is deemed to be healthy. Changes are usually due to alteration in the ecology or climatic variations.

- Some plant species are associated with the availability of honey. To assist in the practice of honey gathering, the Todas have noted when different species flower, the kind of honey produced, and also the bees and other insects that pollinate them. This is elucidated in an ancient song that elaborates on when specific flowers are in profusion and the corresponding species of bees that are pollinating them. Today, when climatic changes cause a given tree species to not mass flower at the correct time, the Todas realize that something is profoundly wrong with their ecosystem and that honey is not going to be available that season.

- Some plants illustrate various items that inspired Toda ancestors. For example, the flowers of *Ceropegia pusilla* were used to model the unique cane milk-churning stick. Not only do these endangered flowers look like miniature churning sticks, their tubers are highly nutritious. Similarly, the circular buffalo pens are said to have been inspired by the shape taken by a clump of Gaultheria bushes, a wintergreen used in pain balms. Flowers have also inspired traditional embroidery motifs and song compositions.

- Some species indicate human reaction. Take, for example, *Gentiana pedicellata*, an herb with small flowers that blooms on the grasslands of the Toda heartland called *arkilpoof*. This Toda name means "the worry flower" and the flower indicates human anxiety levels. The flower carpets the grassland and sometimes it is difficult to walk without treading upon these delicate blooms. It is believed that if a person with worries plucks this plant and holds it without touching the flower, the flower closes. It is very sensitive and closes faster if the degree of anxiety is pronounced. I have found it to be very accurate; when a person with some nagging worry accompanied me, this flower would close in a flash. As long as such species are present at the right period and continue to show the correct reactions, the ecosystem is normal. Since most such plants are hygrophytes, that is they grow in moist places, climatic changes leading to variation in monsoon intensity have lead to their scarcity in many areas.

- The Todas depend upon certain plants for their flowers to indicate not only the season of the year, but also the time of the day. One prominent example of this is the six o'clock flower (*Oenothera tetraptera*) that blooms at almost exactly that time in the evening regardless of weather conditions.

- Certain species mark time and a person's age. The Todas have knowledge of flowering cycles and the medicinal qualities of several *Strobilanthes* species. The general class is called *katt*, with *tehrrverykatt* flowering once in six years, *pelil(zh)ykatt* every twelve years, and *pyoofkatt* every eighteen years. This is also used to denote a man's age and wisdom; a man is said to be extremely wise if he has witnessed several flowering cycles of *pyoofkatt*. In the past, this species was present around every hamlet, and therefore people who had seen it flower twice would know that they were thirty-six years old, and so on. Now, with rapid alteration in the ecosystem and changes in climate, a Toda cannot rely on this as an age indicator.
- Certain species indicate the presence of specific pollinators. As noted, this is primarily related to honey gathering. But this knowledge also led to a Toda understanding that an absence or decrease of a particular pollinator would mean that the corresponding plant species would also diminish in the following season. The absence of the pollinator is typically due to alteration of habitat, use of pesticides, or climate change.
- Some species, like the bark of the *Meliosma wightii* tree, are sacred temple species that can only be used by a priest. Several thorny plant species are used during ordination ceremonies of the priest to purify him.
- Mass flowering indicates the upcoming wild fruit season.

- Mass flowering indicates the availability of certain useful herbs. For example, the powdered bulb of the *Satyrium nepalense* orchid is consumed as an outstanding energizer, a sort of Toda ginseng. The Toda name of this species, *ezhtkwehhdr*, means bullock horns, which is what these flowers resemble individually when plucked. From a botanical perspective too, this suggests that the Todas were aware of the orchid's uncommon twin-spurred flowers; most orchids have single spurs.
- Certain toxic species are to be avoided. The tubers of cobra plants belonging to the *Arisaema* species are known to be toxic.
- Some species have utilitarian properties. Certain bamboo species are used to make flutes, others are used in the construction of traditional structures, yet others are used to make sacred vessels. Rattan cane is used to make a variety of objects including spears and vessels for honey. Among the plants used routinely by the Todas in their rituals for practical purposes are those of the species *Litsea wightiana*. The thin branches of these are dried and used to make fire by friction; fire cannot be made by any other means at ceremonies. Finally, the species of grasses used for thatching provide prolonged shelter from rain.
- Many of the endemic plants in the upper Nilgiris are unusual and visually striking. There are over a dozen endemic balsams (*Impatiens*) in the Nilgiris, and the Todas are able to associate their absence from certain areas with changes in ecology and climate.
- Some plants are used as wild foods and grains. The edible tubers of the churning stick plant are in this category.

5. By incorporating certain sacred rituals that directly assist in the management of the ecosystem. Traditionally, at the start of every winter, the priests of the highest-grade temples initiate a sacred ritual of setting fire, using ceremonial fire sticks, to certain areas of the grassland. Although this was done for ritual purposes, it also played an important role of managing the grassland ecosystem. With the forest service disallowing the fire rites and changes in climatic conditions, there is an alarming decline of vital species like the endemic *Eriochrysis rangacharii*, which is used to thatch temples.

The second method is by ensuring that the ecosystem, be it shola thicket or grassland, around sacred water sources is preserved. Since the Todas know the specific plant species that conserve the hydrology of these ecosystems, they take special care to see that these species are abundant around water sources. This insulates the water source from the effects of global warming. For example, during the summer it is not unusual in recent times to experience a fairly long period of drought. However, due to conservation of water-retaining species, the sacred streams are still perennial, albeit with less water. Most of these water-retaining species have a complex subterranean sponge effect. A few, like *Oldenlandia verticillaris*, hold the equivalent of jugs of water within their large leaves. It is due to such plants that the western upper Nilgiris has the distinction of being one the few ecosystems where precipitation and area water runoff levels (water yield) are equivalent. The Todas also address the harsh climate controls of the western Nilgiri edge by migrating there during the dry season and returning by the time of the harsh monsoon.

6. By incorporating certain sacred rituals that indirectly assist in the management of the ecosystem, such as the salt-pouring ceremonies performed by priests at all temples during different periods of the year. This ritual, besides the utilitarian aspect of feeding brine to buffaloes, is basically a prayer for an abundance of rain and pasture, and thus milk and other vital natural resources in the coming months. Ceremonies like these are a plea to the divine to bless and maintain the health of their ecosystem. Failure to perform the salt rites even today is an invitation for climatic changes and resulting ecological ill health. In another ceremony, Todas gather annually on a sacred hilltop to pray for good rainfall and normal climatic conditions. Also, a few Todas claim to possess the ability to chant sacred incantations to bring about localized rainfall or withhold it for a short period.

7. By practicing vegetarianism, an unusual trait among indigenous people surrounded by game.

The Toda Ecological Footprint

The ecological footprint of an average U.S. citizen is 8,000 kilograms of oil equivalent and a CO_2 emission of 20,000 units. Compare this with those of an Indian: 500 kilograms of oil equivalent and an average CO_2 emission of 1,000 units. Of course, in this consumerist monoculture world, one's eco-footprint is directly related to the per capita income (PCI) of the nation. The United States has a PCI of $35,000 USD, whereas India lags far behind at just $700 USD. We realize that if India were to increase its PCI by fifty times, then its eco-footprint would probably also reach 8,000 kilograms of oil equivalent. One can then visualize the impact this growth would have on the ecosystem.

Edward O. Wilson has calculated that for the developing world, including China and India, to reach current levels of the developed world, four planet Earths would be required to sustain this phenomenal growth.

So what is the ecological footprint of a modern Toda? We calculate Toda PCI to be around $300 USD, less than half that of an average Indian. Even today, less than one in every hundred Todas owns a vehicle, including two-wheelers. (Air travel is almost nonexistent.) Compare this with a 1:1 ratio in the United States. Therefore, emission of CO_2 from vehicles is negligible for a Toda.

What about burning wood to supply energy? The Todas rely totally on wood as a source of fuel. While the government is trying to modernize the Todas by providing them with modern housing, their houses remain small and have little cement and more mud. Toda traditional houses are marvels of tribal architecture and can last for many decades, only requiring periodic rethatching. Even when it is bitterly cold or windy outside, these are very warm within. It is important to keep a fire burning as much as possible, as this makes the various components bind into one cohesive unit. Despite having hardly any foundation, they act as natural windbreakers and remain intact even after the most violent storm. They also blend superbly with the undulating terrain and do not stand out like modern houses do in the grassy downs. The entrances are very low and small and this ensures that no enemy or wild animal is able to enter easily.

In the early 1990s, only half a dozen traditional barrel-vaulted Toda houses remained. All except one were situated in migratory hamlets where no other form of housing is allowed. Then one man asked us to obtain government sponsorship for a barrel-vaulted

Toda Ecological Footprint

Less than one out of every 100 Todas owns a vehicle (including two-wheelers).

Air travel is almost nonexistent.

Traditional structures act as a natural windbreak.

Their traditional structures use natural products that are sustainably harvested from a climax ecosystem, renewable, and harvested when mature.

Their traditional structures have the unique property of not emitting carbon into the atmosphere from the wood burned within. Hence these structures are actually able to capture and sequester carbon.

Photo by Tarun Chhabra

Fig. 9.5. Toda Ecological Footprint sidebar. Courtesy of Tarun Chhabra

house, as his ailing father wanted to depart in a traditional house. The rest is history, and over the past ten years, we have approached government and private agencies, asking them to sponsor traditional Toda houses. Today, we have been able to assist in funding more than forty barrel-vaulted houses. The WILD Foundation has sponsored a few. Added to these are scores of existing temples, two conical and the rest barrel-vaulted.

These traditional structures use natural products that are sustainably harvested from a climax ecosystem, where the consumption and emission of carbon are already balanced. The raw materials are renewable and harvested when mature, thus have already served the vital function of capturing carbon during their growth. Also, these traditional structures have the unique property of not emitting carbon into the atmosphere from the wood burned within. These structures are actually able to capture and sequester carbon. They are eco-friendly and should be promoted. These houses require the smoke to be absorbed within all components to bind the various raw materials into a cohesive unit structure

We conclude that the ecological footprint of a Toda is barely traceable on the ground or in the air.

"Unspeakable"

Victoria Hykes Steere,
Anchorage, Alaska

oh voice—be silent,
keep the words from spilling anger, hurt & pain
blessed snow—calm the soul
weary of life—civilized—it kills one prick at a time
ice moves
wolves song echoes across the ice toward home
am lost—so lost
never old, friends of childhood buried deep
our world—melting, blood red dreams.
sea mammals born on ice, snow & songs of hope
voice give thanks
beauty known, life lived, absolute joy & love cover
despair, we are here
laughter mocking anger, laughter replacing hurt, laughter
soothing pain
so very Inupiaq, so very human, so very much alive!

*8th World Wilderness Congress Poetry Contest,
Honorable Mention